ROBERT DAVIES

MW01539227

HOW ARCHITECTURE SPEAKS

—and fashions our lives

By the same author:

OVERSTREET: an urban street development system. (Harvest House) 1973
THE OTHER ONE: a book of satirical drawings. (Harvest House) 1973
20 DRAWINGS : a portfolio of drawings from the model. 1973
ONCE OVER LIGHTLY: a book of verses. 1973
JIBES, JABS, & JEERS: A book of political cartoons and verses. 1987
THE SECOND COMING: A book of cartoons. 1993
KAPUT: A book of cartoons 1993.

Canadian Cataloguing in Publication data

Mayerovitch, Harry, 1910-

How architecture speaks and fashions our lives

ISBN 1-895854-55-5

1. Architecture - Psychological aspects. 2.Architecture - Human factors.
3. Buildings. I. Title

NA2542.4.M39 1996   720'.1'9   C96-940362-3

If you would like a catalogue of our publications, please write to
ROBERT DAVIES PUBLISHING,
P.O. BOX 702, OUTREMONT, QUEBEC, CANADA H2V 4N6
OR E-mail to: rdppub@vir.com

Harry Mayerovitch

HOW ARCHITECTURE SPEAKS

—and fashions our lives

ROBERT DAVIES PUBLISHING
MONTREAL—TORONTO—PARIS

This book may be ordered in Canada from General Distribution Services
☎1-800-387-0141 / 1-800-387- 0172 FAX 1-416-445-5967;

in the U.S.A., from Associated Publishers Group,
1501 County Hospital Road, Nashville, TN 37218

dial toll free ☎1-800-327-5113;

or call the publisher, toll-free throughout North America:
☎1-800-481-2440, FAX 1-888-RDAVIES

e-mail: *rdppub@vir.com*

Visit our Internet website:
http://rdppub.com

The publisher takes this opportunity
to thank the Canada Council and the Ministère de la Culture du Québec
for their continuing support of publishing.

To Betty Ann

and

to the McGill University School of Architecture
- *now celebrating, in 1996, its Centennial -*
where I was first made aware of the intimate relationship
of architecture to all aspects of our lives.

CONTENTS

WHAT IS A BUILDING ?
7

HOW DO WE PERCEIVE A BUILDING ?
17

WHAT CAN A BUILDING SAY ?
23

HOW DOES A BUILDING SPEAK ?
39

HOW IS A BUILDING MADE ?
83

WHERE IS A BUILDING PLACED ?
135

WHAT IS A GOOD BUILDING ?
155

YOU AND ARCHITECTURE.
177

WHAT IS A BUILDING ?

INTRODUCTION

What is architecture? It is a process for planning buildings and their surroundings to better house and protect the various activities that make our lives possible. In this respect, like other skills such as science and medicine, architecture is essential to survival. Since meaningful survival involves satisfying all our needs - physical, emotional, spiritual - architecture must respond effectively to all of these demands. We may sometimes feel that the expertise this entails is beyond our power or right to question or influence and we are inclined to leave it to the "experts". On the other hand we may simply stand aside and take our architectural environment for granted.

The purpose of this book is to explore what architecture does to be successful and how it can simplify, enrich or complicate our lives.

If we can sharpen our own awareness of the buildings we see or inhabit, we may enhance our enjoyment of them. In short, we can find out how architecture speaks to us.

We may also gain a sense of our own ability and responsibility in determining the kind of buildings with which we may be blessed or cursed.

Let us start with a simple, perhaps over-simple, example.

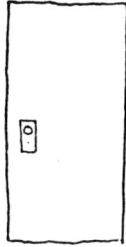

This is a door. It tells us to come in or keep out. Its size suggests that we are able to pass through it easily and the doorknob tells us how.

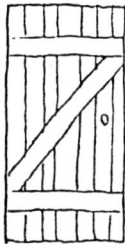

This door tells us how it is constructed - vertical boards held together by cross-pieces and a diagonal brace to keep it from sagging.

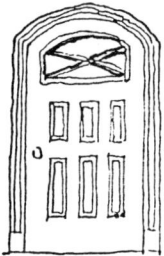

This door tells us by its elaboration that it is important, and suggests that what is behind it is probably important too.

These three doors have spoken to us.

A door not only admits us to a building but also to a world of the senses, the mind and the heart. Doors, together with windows, stairs and balconies, combine to produce something which speaks and at times even sings. The result is a building PLUS - that is to say, a work of architecture.

What can a building say or sing about? Whatever we, as individuals or as a society, want it to. It can tell about our powers, our dreams, concerns, fears, hopes - whatever can contribute to our present or future welfare. What we build will then combine with what we carve, paint, sing or write in order to learn from our past, to enrich our present and to project our future.

However, before a building can speak it must do: it must function efficiently, be accessible and fit into its neighborhood. It must help us cope with the problems of day-to-day living. Only then can the functional and the inspirational combine in an expressive duet.

This book, then, is about shelter, not only as protection, but as a vehicle for further understanding our world and revelling in it.

A little knowledge of the building's language - its grammar and vocabulary - will enable its song to ring more clearly in the ear, and even permit us, the listeners, to contribute to the chorus.

Shelter in nature

Shelter abounds in nature.

The snail and the turtle **are** indeed their own shelters.

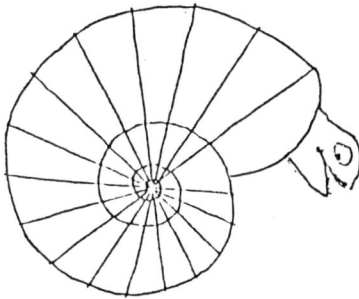

The nautilus shell as it grows, even adds cells to its house to keep it afloat.

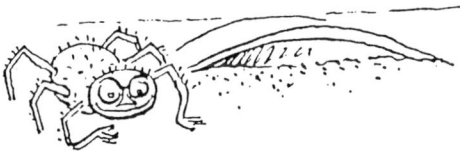

Spiders, bees, beavers devise shelters which double as traps, storage units, or dams.

To ensure their survival these creatures have had to determine for their structures -

- the best location
- the best material
- the shortest construction time
- the least amount of effort required
- the most efficient building method.

Thus, to build its web, the spider sparingly extrudes slender threads from its own body. To store its honey the bee compacts a cluster of wax cells to achieve the greatest volume within the smallest possible enclosing wall area. We cannot but admire the ingenuity and appropriateness of these structures - their order, economy, geometry, rhythm, texture and color, and we therefore pronounce them "beautiful".

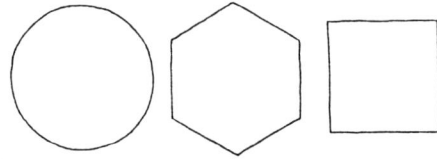

The perimeter of each of these shapes is equal. But the enclosed area of the hexagon is 1.15 x that of the square, of the circle 1.2 x that of the square. But when placed side by side each wall of the hexagon serves its adjacent area, thus becoming more economical than the circle. Hence the bee's wisdom in choosing this construction method for its honey storage cells.

- physical strength and dexterity.

- power to think and reason.

- emotions or the ability to feel.

Shelter by humans

The marvellous structures devised by the animal kingdom accommodate a fixed life style and slowly changing conditions.

We humans however, who are physically ill-equipped to resist excessive cold or heat, damp or drought, or the hostility of competing creatures, have chosen instead a changing and mobile life style. We succeeded in so doing only with the help of ingenious con-trivances, including varied kinds of shelter.

To master the necessary know-how of survival we had much to learn about the physical world and we have had to acquire special capabilities.

The evidence of the earliest hunting weapons, cooking utensils, clothing and dwellings reveal other qualities. Their shapes and decoration go beyond the obviously useful. They suggest purpose, delight and pride. We have continued over aeons to develop this ability to define ourselves, proclaim our powers, project our hopes.

This results in the magic thing we call "art". It is powerfully demonstrated in buildings.

A simple example: even the most primitive communities establish a physical centre or rallying point from which to organize protection, assign tasks, take decisions, celebrate achievements or mourn losses.

14

A tall pole rising out of a building and visible from afar, could designate such a central meeting place.

Elaborated, as in an Indian totem pole, the group's beliefs, history, achievements are made eloquently evident.

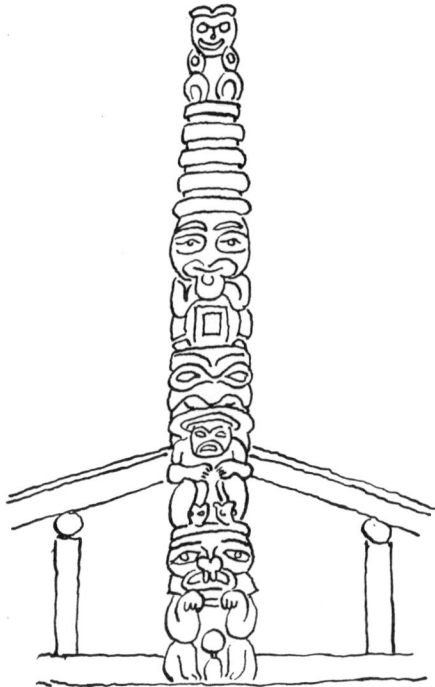

We, their descendants, have inherited the abilityand the inclination to endow even the simplest building with a vision of ourselves. Our homes, for instance, usually reflect our celebration of the family or reveal our special interests. Our gardens proclaim our precious link with nature.

We would also like our homes to persuade ourselves (and others) of our uniqueness and, as our "castles", to give us a feeling of safety.

Different house styles point to different life styles, define our social or economic status, and thus our identity and individuality.

More imposingly, a cathedral can invite us to penetrate the infinite - if we aspire to the eternal. The dimly lit nave serves as a metaphor for the darkness of earthly existence, the resplendent altar the symbol of ultimate release and revelation. Thus architecture becomes a powerful and sophisticated way to proclaim what we are, what we have been and where we hope to go. Put another way - when a building simply shelters and protects, it speaks in **prose**; when it stirs us with hope or memories, it soars to **poetry**.

"We build not only to house our bodies", someone has said, *"but also to house our dreams."*

16

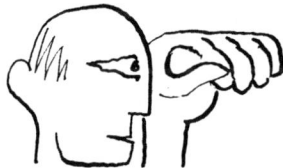

HOW DO WE PERCEIVE A BUILDING ?

HOW DO WE PERCEIVE A BUILDING?

To survive, we try to understand the world, adapt it to our needs, and explore its possibilities. We attempt to perceive it as completely as possible.

We look at a building for similar reasons - to recognize whether it can serve our physical needs and whether we can enjoy what it offers.

To achieve this understanding we are blessed with a highly sophisticated set of faculties, namely -

18

Our senses

which reveal the building's physical properties:

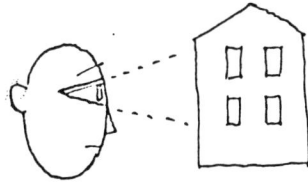

■ **Sight** reveals its location, size and shape.

■ **Touch** tells us it is rough or smooth warm or cool.

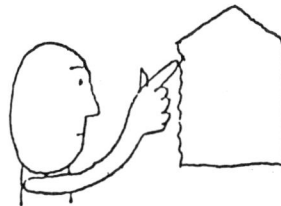

■ **Hearing** reveals the space as hollow, crowded, vast or intimate.

■ **Smell** hints at the kind of activities within.

19

Our reason

which helps us understand the appropriateness of the building's spaces and
forms, and to appreciate (or decry) the
logic of the arrangements.

Our emotions

which tell us how the building has made
us feel. How intensely we feel will be
emphasized by such physical clues as
body temperature, heart beat and muscle
tension. How we will react will depend
on what attitudes we bring to the building. The adventurous in us may seek
surprise; the rational in us order and
structural logic; the self-doubting grand-
iosity or opulence.

But whatever our predisposition, a fine structure can impose an emotional, even irresistible, spell - quiet in a library, exhilaration in a night club, curiosity in an exhibition hall, security and comfort in a home. Notre Dame Cathedral, for example, will overawe, an Egyptian pyramid will overwhelm, the Taj Mahal will hypnotize us into serenity, the Golden Gate Bridge will stun us with its daring.

A BUILDING CAN

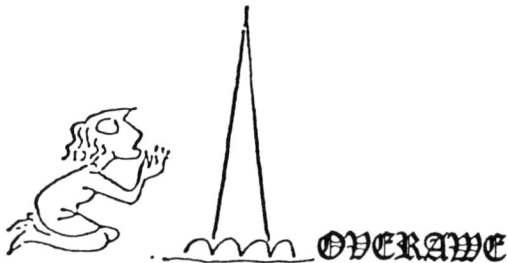

SURPRISE

Charm

Soothe

AMUSE

PUZZLE

INTIMIDATE

OVERAWE

REASSURE

22

WHAT CAN A BUILDING SAY ?

WHAT CAN A BUILDING SAY?

To relate to our fellow creatures we reveal something of our true selves. Some
of us are effusive, others taciturn. We
seldom expose all aspects of ourselves
and this may even make us more intriguing to others, suggesting that there is
something more to be discovered.

Similarly, a building may initially express
its nature and function only in part, and
await further exploration before revealing
its full significance.

A building has many things to say.

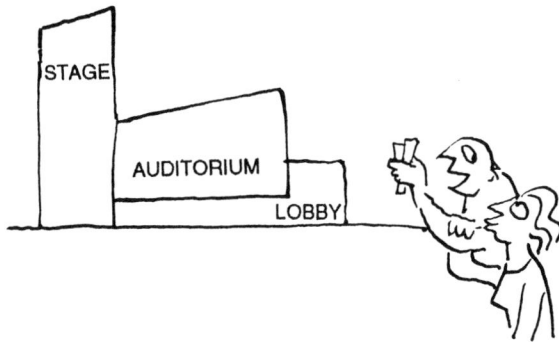

■ It can describe its function.

■ It can explain how it is constructed.

■ It can expose its technical arrangements.

■ It can reveal the social ideas or trad-
itions which inspired its construction.

■ It can, if preserved, re-echo its part
in historic events and claim eternity for
cherished beliefs or achievements.

BOZO
WAS BORN HERE

■ It can, by repeating historical forms,
remind us of the continuity of time.

■ It can speak of the passions and dreams of those whom it shelters.

■ It can debate with adjoining buildings their opposing qualities or proclaim its unity with its neighbors.

■ It can help further a way of life or a political system.

27

The building's language

We humans can communicate with each
other by word - whether spoken, printed,
written or electronically transmitted.   We
also make ourselves understood by body
language. A building speaks to us also
through signs, inscriptions or billboards. It
usually tells us what it is and how it
wants to be understood by its outer clothing - its special kind of body language.
Its variety of gestures enables it to speak
in prose, in poetry, in symbols. Its gestures can assert its dignity, flaunt its daring, or soar into fantasy.

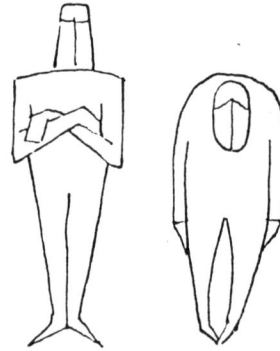

Symbolism

It is clear that no idea or feeling can be
expressed and communicated except
through a tangible form - a poem, a
song, a painting, a ritual.

A Supreme Being can be symbolized by a lamb, a wafer or a sip of wine - their impact intensified when enshrined in a building symbolizing the House of God.

A ruler's control can be symbolized by the radiating avenues in his nation's capitol. (His message can be reinforced if he stations his artillery at the core.)

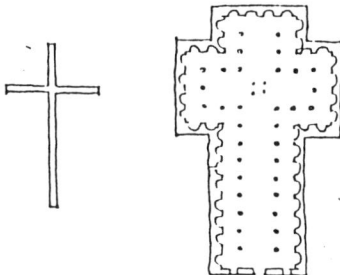

A religious symbol can become the basis for a floor plan

29

Ruined buildings can be valued as symbols of a cherished past. Such relics can be particularly stirring, impressing us with the transitory nature of our lives and works.

Our dependence on water is celebrated in fountains, whose playful jets also proclaim our ability to harness its power.

In the Toronto City Hall, flanking towers housing the municipal and regional governments embrace the central Council Chamber - a symbolic expression of a municipal democracy.

We fear some symbols. In few buildings do we acknowledge the presence of a 13th floor.

Characteristics associated with the male or female sex can also serve as symbols - rugged or fine building details, sharpness or softness of contrasts.

The orderly classic style can symbolize our commitment to the intrellect; the romantic style conveys our trust in the emotions.

Most intimately, our homes symbolize our uniqueness, enshrine our cherished belongings and our special interests. There we can indulge in the nostalgic, and reclaim an idyllic childhood by reconstructing grandma's picket fence with its rows of hollyhocks.

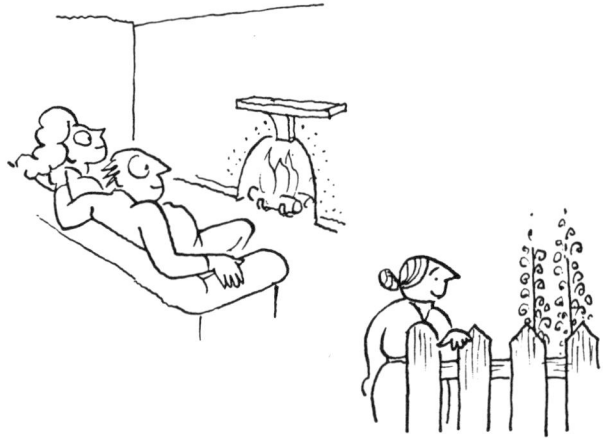

Fire, in the fireplace or in the campfire, is still treasured as a focus for our gatherings and as a visible symbol of its centrality in our life and culture.

Fantasy

From childhood on we create imaginary playmates and worlds, sometimes to express what may be possible, sometimes to escape from the pressures of an imperfect world.

Fantasy transports us into the romantic past, the limitless future or a fairy-tale world of the present. It enlists the perverse, the playful, and the whimsical.

Though literature or painting may permit fantasy full license, architecture is bound by the demands of function, economy and social propriety.

Some fantasy may have originated in the practical world. The corner turret, now a romantic feature, resulted from the need to survey and protect each wall of a building.

The desire for fantasy can be gratified in the wonderland of exhibition buildings - in children's playgrounds or even in one's own backyard.

33

Fantasy is not always an escape. It can generate new insights and new solutions. An old truth, turned on its head, may reveal new possibilities.

LeCorbusier, for instance, had the fanciful notion of transferring the garden from the ground level to the roof of the house, thus adding a few new words to the architectural vocabulary

The home may also be the setting for the surprising and the outlandish - even the irrational. It becomes far more than the purely practical *"machine to live in"*.

Variety

A good meal offers the diner the salty and the sweet, the hot and the cold, the spicy and the bland.   Limited tastes would be boring, possibly even un-healthy. To survive physically and spiritually we need to explore the new, the exciting, the ambiguous, the com-plex, the puzzling and the "yet-to-be-discovered" possible.

Within a single building can be found spaces each of which create different moods - the formality of a dining room, the snugness of a den, the efficiency of a workshop and the irregularity of a storage room.

Individuality within a free society can only be guaranteed by some system of order. In architecture, variety (to avoid confusion or anarchy must be contained within an embracing unity. Such a unity exists in a well-designed shopping mall. *"Freedom,"* said the poet Robert Frost, *"is feeling easy in harness."*

Humor

Humor results from the extreme exaggeration of accepted relationships. It is a highly-charged and short-lived reaction to what may seem like the abandonment of an accepted wisdom or the revelation of a new one.

It is temporary because unlike grief, a smile cannot linger for long. And laughter, if it is not to cause pain, must explode and subside in a few seconds.

36

Most vehicles for humor (a cartoon, a TV skit) are therefore short, pithy, easily absorbed and just as easily discarded in a wastepaper basket or by the twist of a dial.

A building however cannot be so cavalierly treated and therefore its designers must attempt to generate only those emotions that can be comfortably sustained. Few buildings are meant to make us laugh. A fun house in an amusement park can momentarily titillate but a hilarious city hall would negate its serious purpose.

However, humor is not denied architecture altogether. A sudden change of scale or an unexpected color contrast can lighten the mood. A departure

from the expected can elicit a double-
take. The gargoyles in a Gothic cathedral do not endanger its overall ser-
iousness. Michelangelo's columns
(meant to carry a load) unreasonably
and perversely supported on corbels,
make us smile, but only a little.

HOW DOES A BUILDING SPEAK ?

HOW DOES A BUILDING SPEAK?

Architecture is a language with a vocabulary and grammar of its own, a language having much in common with the geometry of nature.

Geometry

Among the devices which nature employs to achieve order, stability and generation is the use of geometric forms, such as the spiral pattern in a seashell or a sunflower. We, as products of nature ourselves, understandably respond to geometric shapes and find comfort in them.

To give our life unity we constantly try to find connections with the harmonies of the universe.

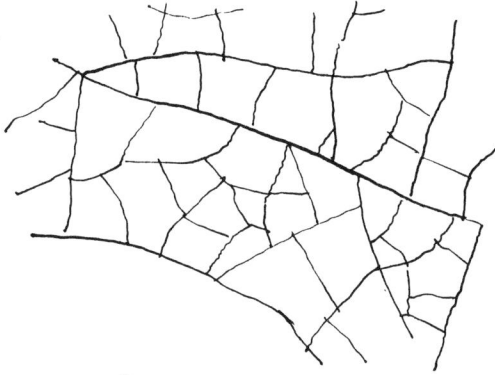

The tendency of the cracks in a parched desert to intersect at right-angles or in the craze of a porcelain bowl, reveals nature's concern for order.

We are uneasy when we see a picture hung slightly askew on the wall, or when a friend's tie is pulled to one side. It is hard to resist straightening them out.

Even in our childhood drawings we tended to reduce complex forms to simple circles triangles and squares.

It is not surprising that the vocabulary of building is made up mostly of regular shapes - squares, rectangles, circles, trapezoids - along with their three-dimensional cousins - cones, cubes, spheres, pyramids and prisms. These basic shapes appearing throughout architectural history proclaim their universality. The shapes are easily grasped by the eye and mind. They suggest that the real world can be absorbed and understood in digestible morsels, and that we need not fear its complexity. They imply a kind of universal order - logical, appropriate, perhaps even preordained.

Each of these shapes, complete and distinctive, can exercise a strong appeal, and the architect will try to assemble them in his building in order to reconcile their conflicting claims on our attention. Unity,

clarity and efficiency require that each element be accorded its appropriate level of importance. To achieve true eloquence some attributes must be stressed, others underplayed. In the words of Gilbert and Sullivan, "*If everybody's somebody, then no one's anybody*".

The grammar

The process of selecting, eliminating and emphasizing the various forms - is called **composition.** It can be considered a kind of grammar.

The forms can be are arranged in many ways - along straight or curved lines, radiating from a central point, interpenetrating each other or one mounted on another. This process need not restrict freedom of expression. Like a chess board, composition establishes limits

43

within which free meaningful movement can develop.

"**Freedom**", said the poet Robert Frost, "*is feeling easy in harness.*"

The grid

One way of achieving unity is to repeat the units within a grid. The repeated use of identical units makes for economy, ease of construction and clarity of expression. It also spares the eye the need to concentrate painfully on each separate element.

Usually the square or rectangular grid offers the greatest flexibility. But the triangular grid, imaginatively exploited by
 Buckminster Fuller in his geodesic struct-

ures, offers great opportunity to create unique structures combining lightness with structural rigidity.

Aside from emphasis, the architect has other means to organise the elements of his buildings for maximum effect on our feelings. These include **scale, rhythm, contrast, harmony, movement, tension, color, texture** and **optical adjustments.**

These resources are the same ones the painter applies to canvas and pigment, the musician to sound and beat and the cinematographer to film and screen. We shall consider each of these elements in turn.

Rhythm

"I got rhythm!" because my heartbeat, and yours, react to the rhythm of the universe.

Night follows day, winter follows summer. We breathe in, we breathe out. We respond irresistibly to this all-pervasive, all-powerful mechanism.

Rocking will put a baby to sleep.

Our feet involuntarily beat time to a lively tune.

Our bodies respond to the rhythm of a hockey player's lunge or a dancer's leap.

We sense how important rhythm is to us when

■ an interrupted rhythm on the dance floor disturbs us.

■ an irregular heart beat threatens.

■ a deviation in our daily schedule annoys.

Without rhythm life is inconceivable. That is why the arts, in order to interpret life, invoke rhythm to reinforce their message.

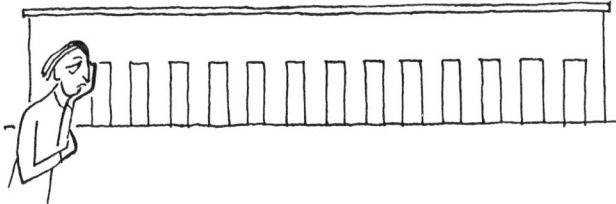

Architecture exploits our sensitivity to rhythm by arranging building elements in orderly sequence.

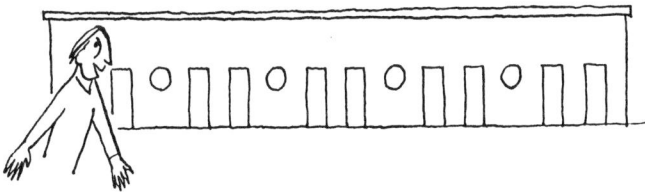

The simplest kind of rhythm is repetition of a single unit.

More complicated and intriguing rhythms involve two or more elements in regular or staggered patterns, ranging from stately to spritely.

Perversely we sometimes resent the power rhythm wields over us. When too insistent, rhythm can be hypnotic and frightening or boring and ineffectual. So we often want to break away, though not so far as to be released entirely from its reassuring influence.

In music, syncopation creates a tantalizing unease, resolved when regular rhythm is resumed. In architecture, a displaced element attracts the eye by its incongruity and provides relief pending resumption of the regular rhythm.

At Pisa, the repeated arch forms unify a complex arrangement of buildings.

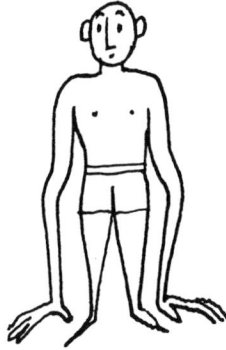

Proportion

A well-proportioned ape has arms that reach the ground. For a human these arms would be a handicap and therefore the person would be ill-proportioned.

We sense the presence of good proportion when the size and shape of an organism or object are in proper relationship to its purpose. A very high ceiling in a small room may make us feel uncomfortable. just as a huge fireplace in a tiny room will make us feel cramped. Good proportion is the fine tuning of the relationship of the parts to the whole.

Is there such a thing as ideal proportion? During certain historic periods there was a tendency to search for ideal principles - absolute, universal, unchanging rules to guarantee perfection in our creations and activities. Architecture has not escaped this magic quest. We have tried to find ideal architectural proportions, some based on the mathematical relationships of the musical scale, others on certain geometrical divisions of space.

The **golden section**, for instance, was a division of space by which the smaller dimension was to the greater as the greater was to the whole. When applied to the floor plans and the facades of a building it was meant to ensure optically satisfying results. Some architects believe that proportion is also affected by color, texture, changing lighting conditions or other accents.

A distorted proportion can be deliberately imposed to attract our attention.

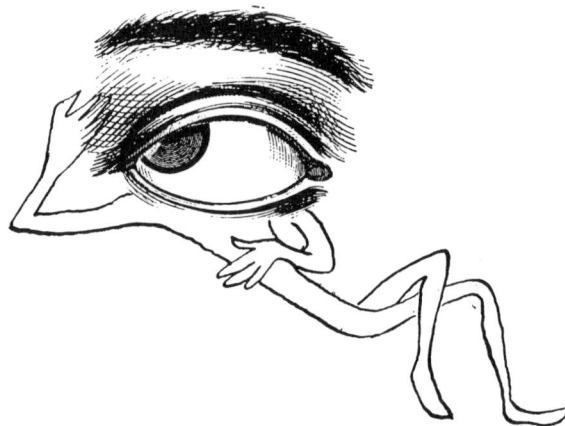

Size and scale

How big is a building? Though useful to know it is not always easy to measure. Its size can be estimated when objects of known size are used as a measuring stick. When you know a brick's height, you can, by counting the number of courses, determine the building's height. We can have little sense of the size of an empty room without the presence of a table or chair to help us determine the **scale**, that is the **relative size**.

The human body has always been a most convenient measuring stick, to determine both size and scale.

A horse is 15 **hands** high.

A pace is 3 **feet** long.

A shot of scotch may be 3 **fingers** high.

A building's height can be roughly estimated by comparing it with our own bodily height. A doorway, usually a bit taller than ourselves, can therefore serve equally well, or a fence railing whose height we are familiar with. When the elements of a building are related to normal human dimensions the building is said to be in **human scale.**

There can be other clues. The eye can estimate distance more easily if the space is divided into equal units - by evenly spaced columns or floor tiles of known size. These repeated units, or **modules**, make the scale of the building apparent.

A large uncomfortable space can be made more acceptable if its scale is **increased**. A small space can be made to appear larger if its scale is **reduced**. The architect is therefore deeply concerned with the scale, since it helps us define our relationship with the building.

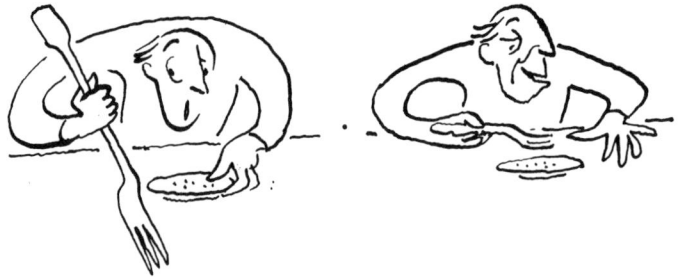

This fork is the wrong size and not in scale with its intended use.

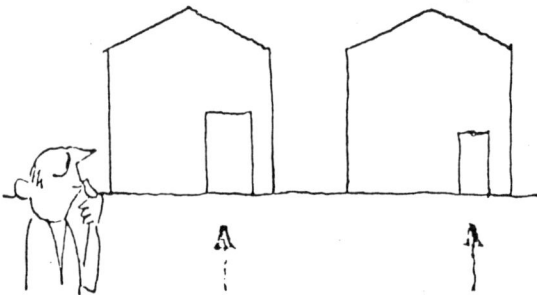

This door makes the building seem *smaller*.

This door makes the building seem *larger*.

The traditional Japanese tatami, a floor mat roughly the size of a reclining human, determines the dimension of the rooms and makes their size easy to estimate.

If all the elements conform in scale there will be repose. An unexpected change of scale will confuse or shock or amuse.

Contrast and harmony

Round versus square, tall versus short, dark versus light, noisy versus quiet, rough versus smooth, hard versus soft, sharp versus dull, serene versus restless, concave versus convex, sweet versus sour, many versus few, simple versus complex.

By seeing characteristics in opposition to each other we can more easily identify objects, tastes and feelings. In short, they make all aspects of our lives easier to understand. Two buildings will seem to

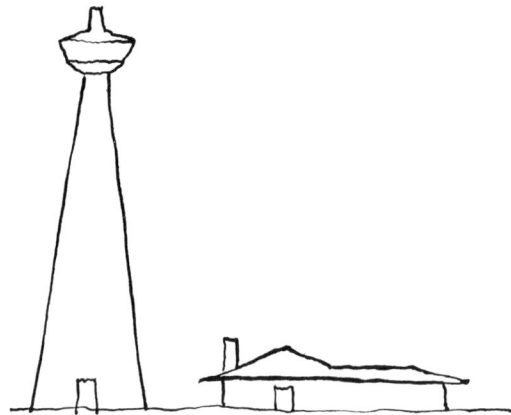

A tower seems taller when an adjacent building is low.

56

be related to each other when their size or color or texture are similar. When they have contrasting qualities we recognize their individuality.

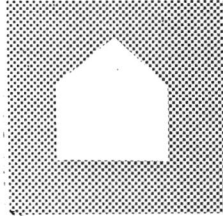

Contrasts attract. Unexpected or extreme contrasts will create a shock. A white area on a black background will catch the eye sooner than a white area set against a light grey background. For that reason the eye will move from lesser to greater contrasts and come to a climax at the point of highest contrast. Buildings therefore can be thought of as being composed of contrasts designed to achieve emphasis and unity.

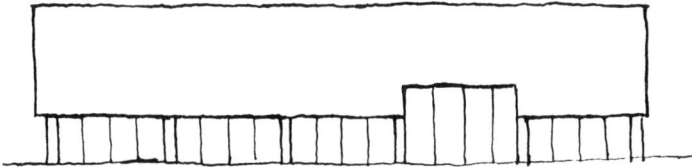

The interruption of the horizontal continuity by a contrasting break is meant to stress the location of the building's entrance.

Symmetry

The earth remains in balance by revolving about its central axis.

A turtle crawls, a bird flies and a human runs because their bodies also are balanced about a central axis. Even though the axis may not be visible its presence is nevertheless sensed.

Since our eyes and our ears are symmetrically placed, we can gauge distance and pinpoint the source of a sound.

We feel a building is in balance when its elements are arranged symmetrically. Then it appears to be in repose - fixed and inevitable. We are tempted to move toward its main entrance along its central axis.

Symmetry is one of the elements suggesting that the building may have a formality of purpose which would merit a formality of attitude.

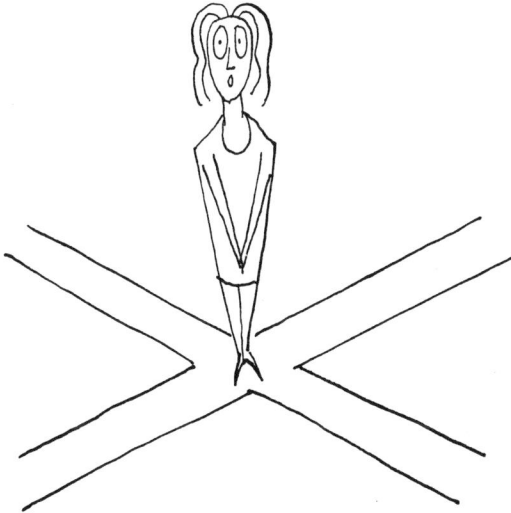

Symmetry along two or more axes pins us down even more compellingly. For that reason the intersection is a frequently chosen spot for an important feature - an obelisk, a fountain or a statue. Building complexes and even cities have been located at great intersections to emphasize their strategic importance.

Asymmetry

Balance can also be achieved asymmetrically. A small object can balance a larger one, if it is intense in color, unusual in shape or placed at an appropriate distance from the axis.

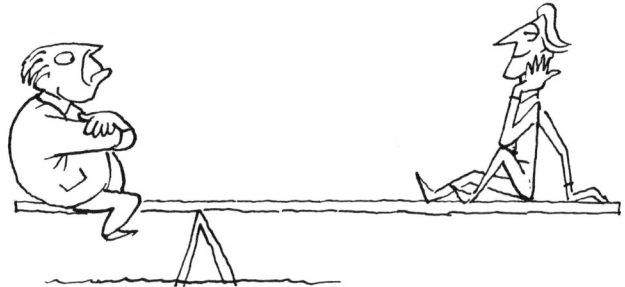

An asymmetrically arranged building can help suggest that it is dedicated to informal activity. It encourages freer direction of movement within and without and can help induce a more easy-going attitude on the part of visitors or occupants.

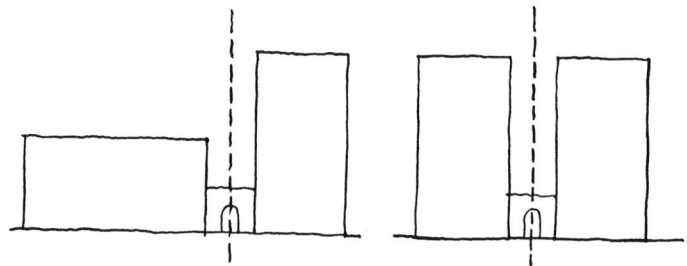

Achieving balance is not always the designer's intention. He may wish perversely to create a deliberate imbalance to keep us on edge or in motion.

Symmetry tends to prevail in static times; asymmetry in periods of change.

Sculptural form

Sculpture is a three-dimensional interpretation of life. Children recognize this
when they pile one block upon another.
Since we ourselves are three-dimensional
creatures, anything sculptural suggests a
reality and a substance which is reassuring

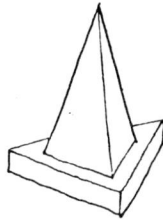

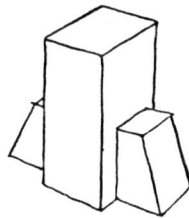

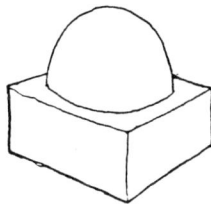

A building can be seen as sculpture,
whether as one geometric form or as an
assembly of cubes, cones, cylinders and
spheres. These may envelop, buttress or
interpenetrate each other to provide an
infiinite vocabulary to the designer.
Abutted or superimposed, each sculptural
form can maintain something of its own
identity or, in combination with others,
make up an intricate whole.

61

While color can enrich, most buildings are monochromatic, depending on solidity and purity of form for their effect.

Though the sculptured forms can be interesting in themselves, they can sometimes take on symbolic meaning - the hemisphere suggesting the heavens or the sphere the perfect completeness of the universe. Their emotional effect can range from the delicate (as in a minaret) to the forbidding (as in a fortress).

To appreciate the building as sculpture the eye can be helped as follows:

■ by softening the transition from one plane to the next,

■ by suggesting the existence of a feature just around the corner,

■ by creating a transparency which reveals the building's depth.

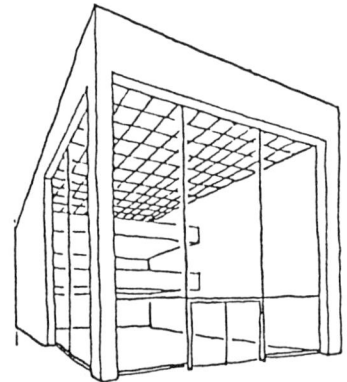

The Boston City Hall - a complex sculptural arrangement.

Independent works of sculpture can supplement the architecture. There have been periods when sculpture and architecture (and painting too) have been so intertwined that they seem to dissolve into each other.

New structural methods such as cable systems or membrane enclosures, can produce light, tensile, transparent sculpture.

When the wholeness of the volume is interrupted by a brutal extrusion or extraction, we experience sculptural shock.

Two similar elements placed beside each other create a dignified duality.

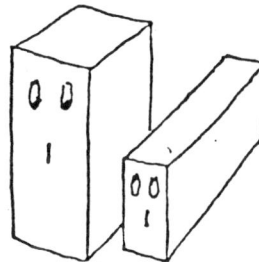

Two dissimilar elements interact more dynamically.

Interpenetration makes for a more intimate bond.

63

Texture and surface

Our fingers linger on the smoothness of
silk or the seductive pull of velvet, but
they shrink from the scraping of a sheet
of sandpaper. Texture reveals a surface
to our touch - it attracts or it repels. Even
if we do not actually touch the building
our experience of surface textures can
declare it friendly or hostile, seductive or
repelling, delicate or strong.

*A hard granite bench
discourages
a prolonged rest.*

*A velvet sofa
asks us to linger*

*A rough concrete
surface can make
the fingers bleed*

*A waxed polished
mahogany wall
invites a caress.*

Optical corrections

Magicians know that our senses and emotions can easily be deceived because we prefer to see what we want to see or what we expect to see.

Eyewitnesses to a crime, for instance, often misinterpret the event or wrongly identify the wrongdoer because of emotional stress. The context of the event can color the event itself.

As an example - this illustration can be read as a white vase against a dark background or as two bears facing each other against a light background. The interpretation will depend on where the eye places its emphasis.

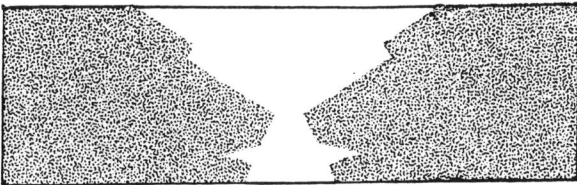

Similarly, visual misinterpretations can result in a distorted view of a building.

65

The architect can deliberately create a visual misunderstanding or take steps to prevent it.

The ancient Greeks spared no effort to correct optical aberrations to achieve perfect visual satisfaction, .

The Disappearing Hat Trick

■ To correct the apparent sag in the middle of a long horizontal line they humped it.

■ To correct the apparent concavity in a long vertical line of a column they caused it to swell slightly along its length. This they called the **entasis.**

66

Today our need to manufacture mass-produced identical building units makes such subtle refinements difficult.

Other visual ambiguities -

A mirrored skyscraper reflecting the opposite side of the street gives it a puzzling insubstantiality.

A too-realistic mural can create a non-existent space

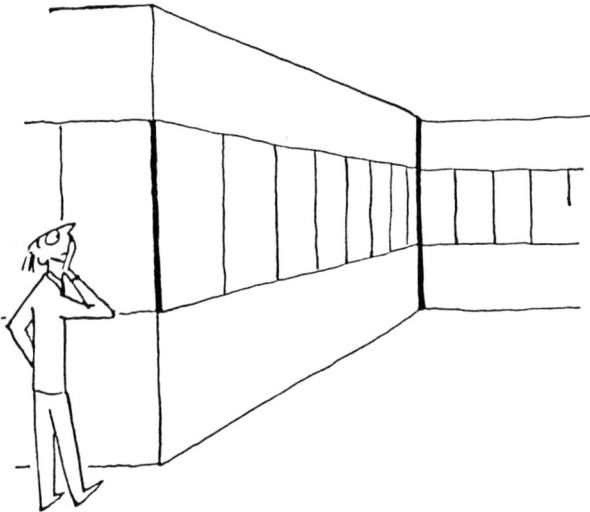

Believe it or not - the two heavy vertical lines are the same length. When seen in perspective the relative size of objects can be deceptive.

68

Light

Without light a building can be said to disappear. Light alone will reveal it. As light changes, so will the appearance of the building. Daytime with its single light source will define clearly, twilight will soften, and night will obliterate. At different times of the day the changing light will describe the building differently, each hour giving it a different face.

For example -

If the sun strikes the building from a noon-day high the shadow in a door or window recess will be deep, thus suggesting a thick wall.

If the building directly faces the light source the shadows will be thinner and will suggest a thinner wall.

If the building faces north or if the day is cloudy, shadows will be weaker and will suggest a thinner wall.

These constant changes will induce a variety of moods. Sharp light and shadow will generate lively reactions. Diffused softer forms will produce gentle, even melancholy states of mind.

Seen from outside at night, the building's interior lighting will reveal a dimension not seen in daytime. The building seems turned inside out, its exterior a disembodied silhouette.

Light in the building's interior, usually stemming from a variety of artificial sources, produces a range of color and intensity. The results are by design restful or stimulating, warm or cold.

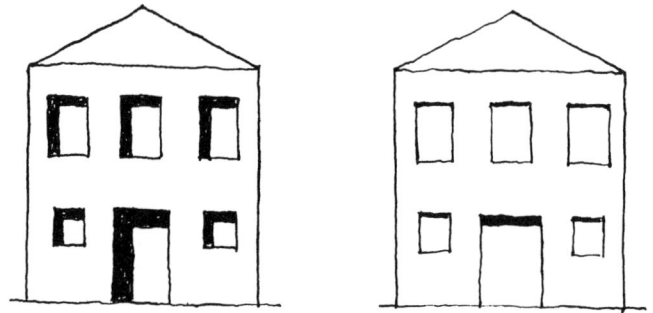

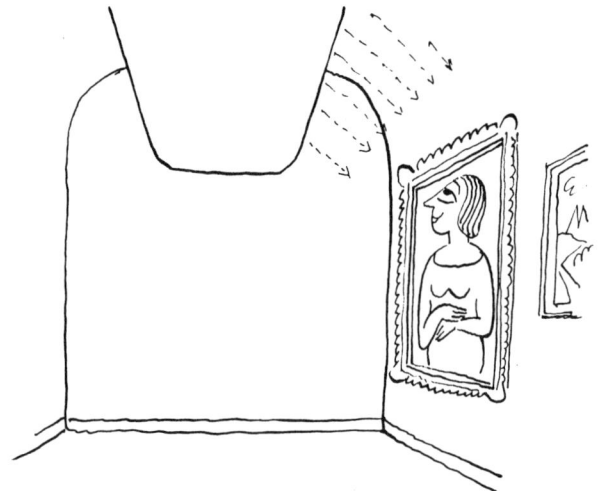

The soft, even, controlled lighting in a museum adds a serenity to the picture viewing experience.

A restaurant's low candlelight will flatter facial complexion by eliminating the hardness and depth of the shadows under the eyes.

Strong flashing colored lights in a discotheque will produce the desired frenetic mood.

Hard monotonous office lighting may lead to inattention, boredom or depression.

Sound

Sound, when manipulated as noise or music (or silence) is a powerful generator of emotion. It is intimately related to architectural space such as in

- the swelling reverberations of an organ or choir within a church - or

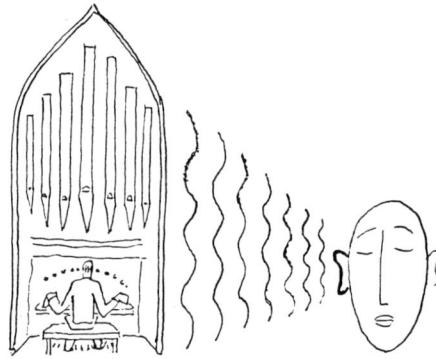

- the tinkle of water in a park fountain - or

- the chilling clatter of horses' hooves on a cobbled rain-drenched street in a Sherlock Holmes movie - or

■ the hush before the arrival of the soloist on the concert stage

By shaping the building enclosure and modifying its surfaces the projected sounds can be diffused, concentrated or softened.

■ A whisper in a circular space will be heard distinctly around the perimeter.

■ A hard- surfaced wall, ceiling or floor will create sharp reverberations

■ A soft surface, such as carpetting or sound-absorbing ceiling tiles, will have a muffling effect and even coax us into subdued tones or silence.

Ornament

The first "decorators" were plants and
animals. Over centuries their form took
on specific colors and patterns, enabling
them to identify their kin, confuse their
enemies or attract the opposite sex. The
precise kind of adornment of the various
species was influenced by their specific
nature, their process of reproduction, their
environment - in short, their relatively
fixed life style.

The body builds and adornment of humans are more specifically oriented to a
mobile life style than to a fixed way of
life. Consequently, they have had to devise added decoration, when necessary to
attract, repel, protect or conceal.

■ They have had to don a lion's skin to conjure up superhuman strength or wear a crown of eagle's feathers to magically invoke great speed or

■ adorn their bodies with clothing, cosmetics and decorations to suggest power, sensitivity, taste, wealth or individuality.

Humans like to adorn what they adore.
■ They clothe their fellow creatures attractively - or

■ They invest the objects they possess or use with alluring qualities - or

- They house their activities in an appealing environment

- They like to elaborate their art

  · in music - with trill and cadenza

  · in poetry - with adjective and alliteration

  · in calligraphy - with serif and curlicue.

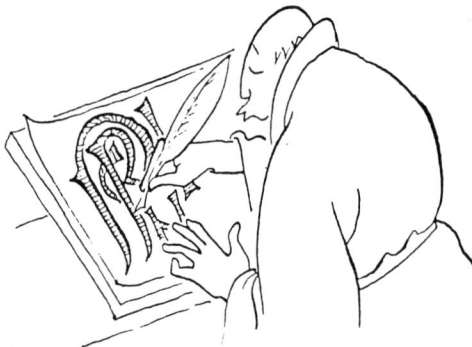

"With witchcraft of his wit,

with traitorous gifts

O wicked wit and gifts ......"

Buildings are obvious objects of this attention, as they provide the most enduring and most visible opportunities for decoration - to express joy in living, homage to wealth or power, or spiritual unity.

Building decoration can be further enhanced by the addition of symbolic elements, including the human figure itself.

It is in this light that we can best appreciate Ruskin's declaration that ornamentation was the principal part of architecture. This view has been echoed more recently by "post-modern" architects who declare that ornament is the real function of the facade, that the building is simply a "decorated shed"

At the same time, some architects have minimized the significance of ornament. Yet it cannot be denied that the complete absence of decoration, as in an empty room, would provide little hint of the room's purpose or the character of its occupants. Ornament adds texture and enrichment even in its simplest form.

Over-elaboration can suggest an ostentatious display.

The importance of ornament is emphasized when the effort and expense involved in its production are evident. Machine-made repetition is less persuasive than laborious and lovingly executed hand carving or painting.

The imaginative and loving fretwork of a 19th century house is ornament at its most playful.

When given the priority, the ornamentation can completely cover a wall or ceiling or floor, as may be seen in an Islamic mosque or behind a Mexican altar.

As stillness provides an important setting for the actor's soliloquy and listening is an appropriate addition to the conversationalist's vocabulary - so can ornament be particularly effective when confined to selected areas set off against a blank background.

COLOR

The red rose attracts the hummingbird to its nectar.

The brightly colored plumage of the male attracts the female bird.

The drab color of the sitting hen conceals it from a predator.   No "sitting duck" she!

The green snake in the green grass confuses prey and predator alike.

The red-yellow-green traffic lights prevent accidents.

Read: color helps us survive.

Color also affects our moods. Light colors cheer us up; dark colors depress us. Soft colors can soothe; strong ones arouse us.

The warm yellow of the sun is likely to stimulate, the cool blue or violet of the night, relax. We **"feel blue"**, we **"see red"** or we view the world through **"rose-colored"** glasses.

Colors are not seen in isolation. They affect each other by setting up degrees of contrast. They minimize or stress differences.

Colors of extreme contrast (that is, **complementary** to each other) - red and green, yellow and violet, orange and blue - tend to accentuate each other. At their most intense they will irritate the eye, a condition only overcome by keeping them apart or separating them with a neutral area (grey, white or black) or by reducing the intensity of one or both colors.

Intense colors will seem closer to us, muted ones seem to recede. Adjacent colors - red, orange, yellow - blend and harmonize with each other and thus put less strain on the eye .

One color cannot be said to be superior or more beautiful than another, but they can affect each of us differently. Sometimes we have preferences related to special associations. Green, for instance, may be a girl's favorite color because it sets off her red hair.

Colors have also been accorded symbolic meaning because they are so emotionally powerful. The yellow of the sun symbolizes life and joy. Our helplessness in the dark leads us to associate black with fearsome things like death. These symbols are not necessarily universal. White symbolizes mourning for the Japanese, for instance, while Indian brides wear red.

Color can conceal or highlight a building, contrast it with its setting or blend it into the background.

The green grass of summer may accentuate the redness of the building's brick. The white of winter provides a neutral background against which many colors can co-exist without friction.

Rain or the weathering of time can change a building's color. The haze of dawn will grey it down, the noonday sun will intensify it, the evening sunset cast an orange glow, the dark night reduce all to a ghostly purple silhouette.

The architect can often moderate or intensify the relationship of the building color to its surroundings. A neutral gray for the building material will allow full play to nature's stage lighting. Alternatively, the prevailing grey of the modern city permits, even encourages, strong colour accents in the buildings.

Too many colors can create visual conflict, since they send confusing messages to the eye. The color harmony on a Greek island results from the predominant use of only one building material - a gleaming white stucco which sets off the brilliance of sky, water and vegetation.

Modern artificial lighting can offer the building a change of colour for evening wear.

Stained glass windows will infuse the interior light of a church with an exceptional brilliance and mystery.

HOW IS A BUILDING MADE ?

HOW IS A BUILDING MADE?

Structure

Architectural space is defined by structure. The role of structure is twofold: it encloses the volume of space we occupy and acts as the support for its components - the walls, roof and other elements. The structure must resist the lateral forces of wind and earthquake and the erosion of material brought about by temperature changes and decay. It must also sustain the vertical load of its own weight and that of the building's contents. It can do so by calling upon the inherent strength of the material of which it is composed (stone, brick, wood, metal) and by transferring the loads to the ground through ingenious devices such as arches, buttresses and columns.

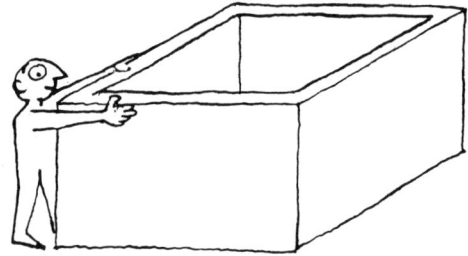

84

In outer space we can thumb our nose at gravity; on earth we can only hope to minimize or divert its force. We cannot resist straining our structures (and our fancy) to the limit.

Even at an early stage in our history we attempted to bridge longer and longer distances. When stones of sufficient length were not available or were too heavy to transport, we developed the ingenious arch form, employing small mutually supporting stones for the purpose.

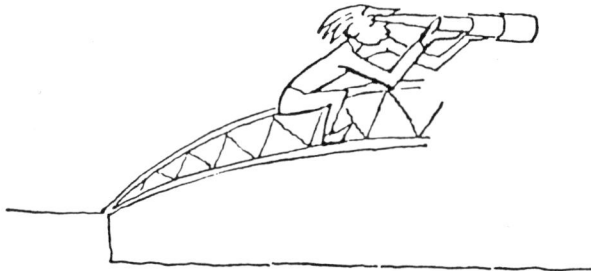

This passion to span larger and larger spaces and reach greater and greater heights continues to challenge us.

Structures now range in size from the simplest beam and column to the more

complicated arches, vaults, domes, can-
tilevers, warped concrete vaulting and
inflatable or suspended roofs. Each
structural system has its own expressive
qualities - one can comfort, another
daunt, still another intrigue with its orig-
inality.

What makes structure expressive?

Because we constantly lift objects or
push them or haul them or throw them,
our bodies have a sense of weight and
thrust. We can imagine the forces
exerted in a building structure and we
react to their apparent strength or weakness. We sense a weight pressing down--
ward and outward and we can guess that
its thrust can be contained by buttressing
or by tying it back within the interior.

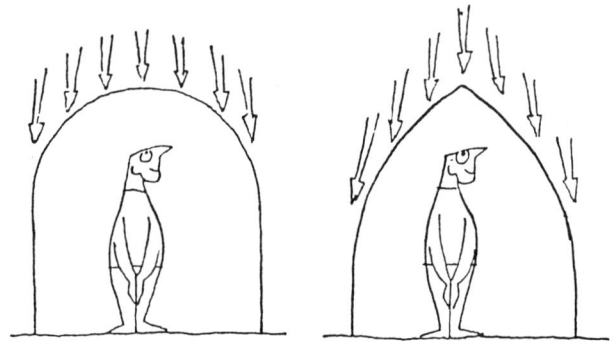

86

The structural load having been diverted to either side of the opening to relieve the lintel, the eye can be assured that the sculptural inset can rest comfortbly without having to absorb any stress.

Though we seldom ask how much a building weighs, our comfort requires that we sense

- that the total load can be supported
- that the accumulating loads can be passed down to their final transfer to the ground.
- that the structure will not topple over laterally.

We do know how to calculate the stresses and how to counterbalance them so that the building is structurally adequate; but for our complete reassurance it must **appear** to be adequate.

We see how nature deals with some of these powerful forces.   A tree withstands uprooting by thickening its trunk

87

at the base to resist both tensile and
compressive stresses. Without a similar
device a building might seem to be in
danger of sinking into the ground. So to
reassure the eye we can

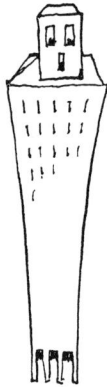

■ broaden the base of the building.

■ expose the structural system to
display its adequacy.

■ reveal the thickness of the wall.

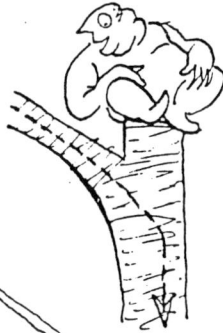

■ add weight to the buttressing to contain the stresses.

■ reveal the direction of the stresses.

■ make the method of construction evident.

Thus, by revealing its presence and adequacy, structure can speak and reassure us.

Structure can also express ideas by association. The pointed arch, for example, has been endowed with spiritual connotations because it arose from the need to increase the width of the naves in Gothic cathedrals. Even today, we find this form more appropriate for a church than for an office building.

Height

From birth we struggle to master the upright posture essential to our survival. Verticality and height have often been equated with self-importance, dignity, aspiration and dominance. It is not surprising that we should wish to express these qualities in our buildings.

The notion of height is most vividly expressed by the **column**. It appears in most cultures, not only as a structural device, but as a revered symbol. Originally appearing as a post, a flagpole or a totem pole, the column attained great eloquence in the ponderous pillars of ancient Egypt. The dignified Doric, the graceful Ionic, and the luxurious Corinthian columns of ancient Greece added further variation and enrichment. The column was accorded the highest ac-

colade when it was converted into the
human form itself - the Greek **caryatid**
and the flankng saints of Gothic cathedral
doorways.

The forked column, whose triangular
shape provides both vertical and lateral
assurance, is a modern variation of the
form.

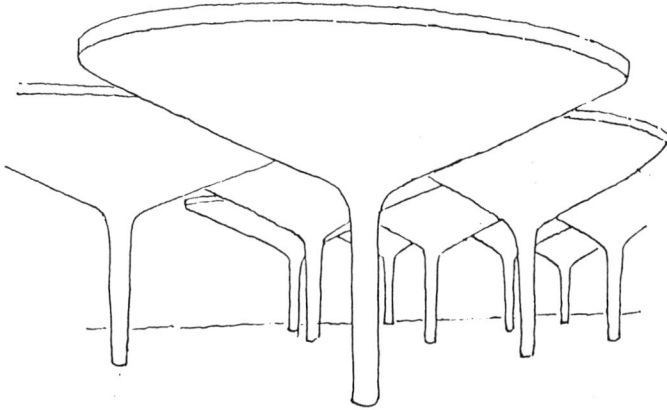

More audacious still is the column with its flaring capital, which accepts some of the responsibilities of the roof.

So endearing is the column that, even when not required for load-bearing, it is flattened against the wall as a **pilaster** to add dignity and richness to the facade.

Skeleton frames

The mastery of height is found most dramatically expressed in the skyscraper, a symbol of our time. It was achieved by the development of a light but rigid structural frame encased in a thin facing material.

The higher the building the greater the challenge to achieve actual and visual stability. (A masonry wall of unusual height would have involved progressive and unwieldy thickening to receive the added load). In the skeleton frame formula, if the *structure* is emphasized its strength is expressed. If the *skin* is emphasized the building seems weightless. If the surface is mirrored the building may even lose its identity and simply reflect the existence of its neighbors.

94

Cantilevers

Nature has provided a mechanism enabling a plant or living creature to extend its reach beyond its root. The branch of a tree reaches beyond its trunk; the human arm stretches away from the body.

The cantilever extends the upper levels of a building beyond its base - a direct challenge to gravity.

An early use of the cantilever - pouring boiling oil on a besieging enemy.

We make bold and even arrogant use of this device in building. Structural daring is a heady measure of power, so we must sometimes be forgiven the occasional pointless muscle flexing.

Suspended structures

Inflated fabric roofs further extend our
structural vocabulary, by emphasizing the
indivisibility of support and enclosure.

Particularly dramatic are thin warped
concrete shells. These, like the eggshell,
contain the inner stresses within the most
precisely calculated thickness of the
structure, assuring the greatest economy
of material, the least possible weight and
the subtlest elegance of contour.

Materials

The earliest building materials were natural products such as wood, stone, reeds and mud. Later, some of these were combined. Mud and straw made bricks; stone, lime and sand made concrete. Still later, even more complex combinations produced tin, steel, aluminum and plastics.

We can usually recognize the nature of a material by its appearance. We are not likely to mistake a plank of wood for a sheet of steel. When we look at a material we assume that it will perform in the way to be expected of that material - whether it will stand up to wear, carry a load, resist twisting, feel warm to the touch or recall for us the spirit of our grandfather's log cabin The more accurately a material reveals what it is, the more satisfying will be its effect on us. If the material seems to be other than what it is, we may doubt its dependibility, making it appear to be pretentious or shoddy or downright dishonest. This doubt can only cause us discomfort and uncertainty.

How a material is used is also important. *"Bricks **want** to form an arch!"* said the late architect Louis Kahn. They wish to exploit their compressive strength and acknowledge their tensile weakness - in short, to be themselves. Do not humans as well desire to achieve that same cap-ability?

Our technical ingenuity enables us to imitate one material with another. Plas-tics, for instance, are often used to sim-

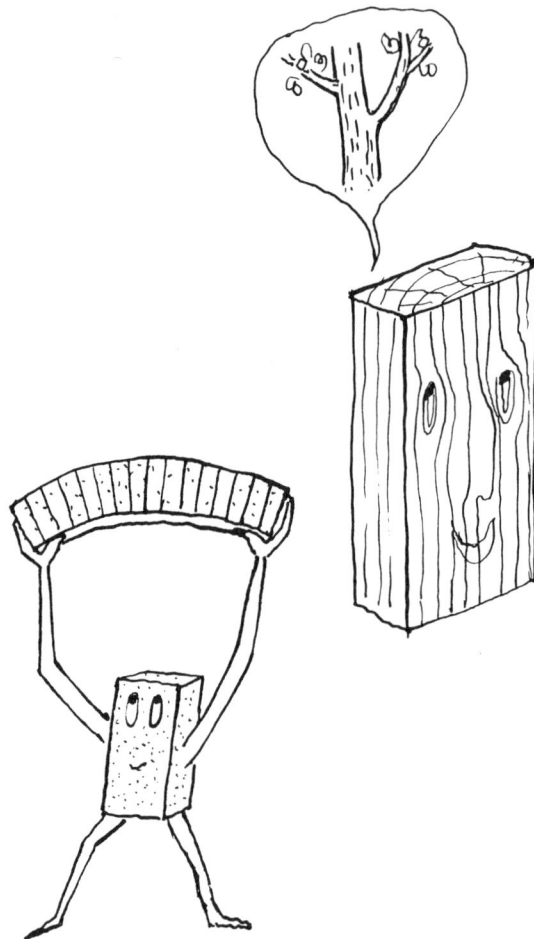

ulate wood, marble or metal, which have distinctly different qualities.

Respecting a material's natural quality lends an integrity and conviction to the building. It reinforces our link with the universe. **Stone** will recall the strength of the mountain; **wood** the resilience and delicacy of the tree.

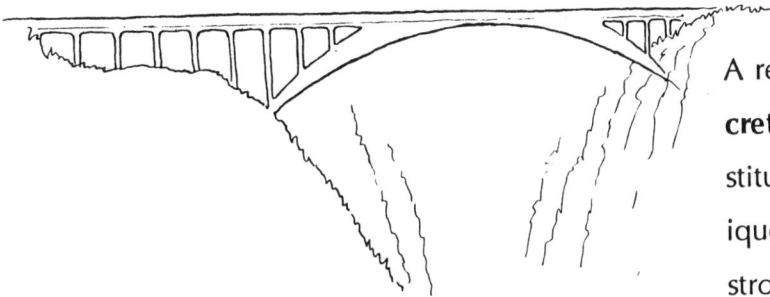

A relatively new material such as **concrete**, once thought of as a good substitute for stone, has finally had its unique qualities respected. Ductile and strong, it can be freely, even expressively, molded to reflect the direction and distribution of its inner stresses. **Glass,** once available only in small pieces, can now be used to build entire walls, thus adding its transparency and strength to the building vocabulary.

New materials are best left to discover
their own voices.

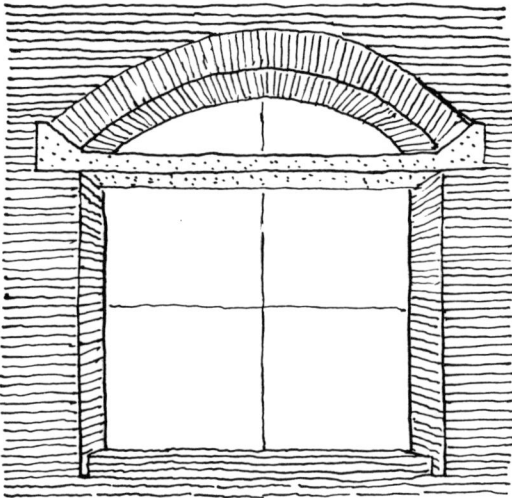

A window lintel by Louis Kahn - where the
compressive thrust of the brick arch is contained
by the tensile strength of the reinforced concrete
tie - each material permitted to display its own
special talent.

Roofs

A judge's wig earns him more respect than his bald pate.

We bare our heads to a crowned superior.

A folded newspaper on the head transforms a child into a general.

Rapunzel's tresses were her crowning glory.

To be capped on graduation day marks the attainment of intellectual accomplishment.

A building too seems to call for a crown - a termination of the movement from base, to body, to top. This sequence parallels the way in which our bodies are organized. We have legs to carry, a trunk to be supported and a head to supervise. The relationship of these three elements seems to suggest that most things have a beginning, a middle and an end. Clear thinking requires a premise, a development and a conclusion, like a play or a piece of music.

It may be said that when we crown a building, we are in effect crowning ourselves.

The roof is a particularly expressive element of the building. It can make a building soar or it can hug the ground, thereby suggesting aspiration or repose. It can be restricted modestly to the limit of the building's perimeter or project far beyond its outer edges to create a sheltering canopy. Hence the appeal of Walt Disney's spires, steeples, towers and minarets, along with their embellishments - the castellations, lookouts, weather-vanes and dovecotes.

The roof's precise shape may also depend on its function. It is sloped gently to shed the rain, or steeply to prevent the piling up of snow. (In some cases the snow is allowed to pile up on a flattish roof to provide insulation against the cold.)

The roof can overhang to protect against the sun in the hot summer and shield against falling snow in the winter.

It can lie flush with the wall to frustrate high winds.

The roof's shape can therefore tell us something of its practical function, while putting a finishing touch to the building's expressiveness.

Towers

The gods dwelt in high places. The fairy-tale princess was rescued from the top-most window in the tower.

Towers are a bold demonstration of our technical reach as we challenge height, wind and earthquakes. Towers signify spiritual or political power. They may also tell of individual or corporate ambition; they have indeed become the most pervasive expressions of our competitive times.

The proliferation of towers in this century robbed height of its distinction - as has their monotonous box-like anonymity. Hence the search by designers for an identifying and individualizing culmin-ation, such as a dome, a sloping roof-line or a classic pediment.

105

Floors

Gravity binds us to the earth's surface - the base of all architectural experience.

No matter how daring our adventures in height and size and complexity our most immediate and intimate sensations of a building are felt through our feet. Even visually our closest contact with a building is its floor. Its design, its horizontality, its spacial subdivisions, its pattern, its color, are all significant.

The floor transmits to the soles of our feet the feel of its every textural variation and deviation from the horizontal.

106

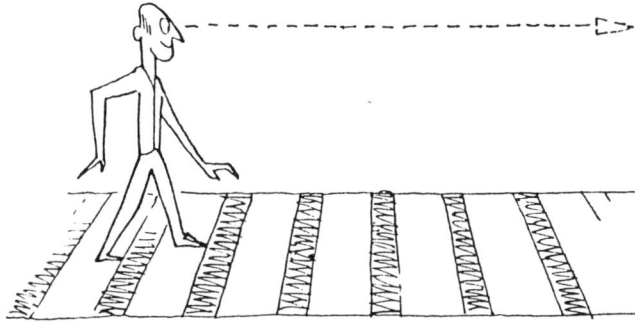

The change of pattern on a floor can create the illusion of separate spaces or even designate a spot for special emphasis.

A steep ramp unbalances us, a granite floor tires, the deep pile of a rug relaxes.

The variations in color, pattern and texture, enrich the walking experience. A floor design can stop us dead, rush us along, invite us to linger, or suggest intriguing directions to explore:
- chevrons, spirals, waves and diagonals, can influence direction.
- contrasts such as squares or checks make us step lively.
- harmonies of color or shape can induce a leisurely pace.
- horizontal stripes suggest continuity - even help gauge distances.

Stairs

While we can explore spacial richness and variation by moving from one area to another, we can add to the effect by moving also from one level to another.

The ramp, and in particular the stairway, offer possibilities for making movement an event - perhaps even feeling as though we are making a transition to another world. The movement may be easy and inviting, or difficult and daunting.

The long steep access to a religious shrine deliberately stresses that spiritual fulfilment involves difficulty and sacrifice.

A gentle incline imparts dignity and elegance to the up or down movement, especially when interrupted by restful landings

A turn in the staircase can hint at an intriguing adventure.

A ramp can strain the body's muscles because of the unnatural angle it imposes between leg and foot. It does, on the other hand, provide convenient access to the disabled.

A gracefully curving stairway can in-
spire the "Grand Staircase Manner".

A double staircase further dramatizes an
ascent but can cause confusion.

The escalator has made the access to another level of the building direct and painless.

The elevator substitutes the drama of the escalator's gradual ascent with that of close encounters.

Doors

The door is the entry point of the building - signalling an invitation to an inner world. For this reason it receives in most buildings the greatest emphasis. The invitation may be whole-hearted as in a movie house. It may be less obvious as in the side entrance of a residence.

A transparent glass door invites visually before it admits physically.

A cruel door! - steel bars suggest invulnerability, openings encourage fantasies of freedom.

The door may perversely deliver a double message, both inviting and repulsing, as in a bank - suggesting at one and the same time that it welcomes customers, but assures that it is difficult for a would-be robber to enter.

A door knob beckons, especially at hand height and placed to one side indicating the direction of the door swing. On the other hand, if the knob is at the centre of the door and higher than convenient to the hand, it will emphasize the building's importance rather than the ease of entry.

The same doorway can be adapted to
serve more than one purpose -

■ a ceremonial entrance for grand
occasions - within which is a modest
access for everyday use.

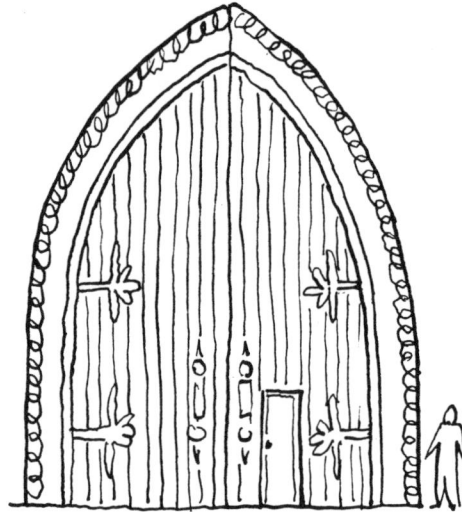

■ a door for all seasons

■ a flap for Fido.

114

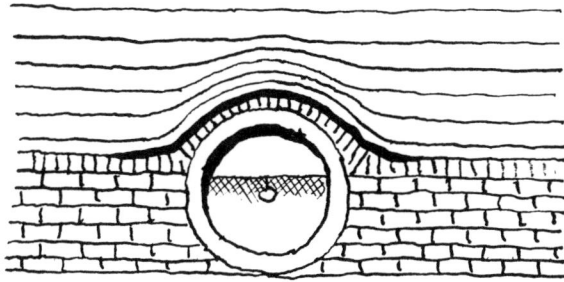

Windows

Windows are the eyes of the building. They are as expressive as human eyes - peculiar two-way eyes revealing and admitting the outside world. Windows unite the interior with the exterior in a welcoming embrace or a stand-offish co-existence. They admit light, sun and air. Their size, shape and location are suited to the climate, the space they serve, the area they view.

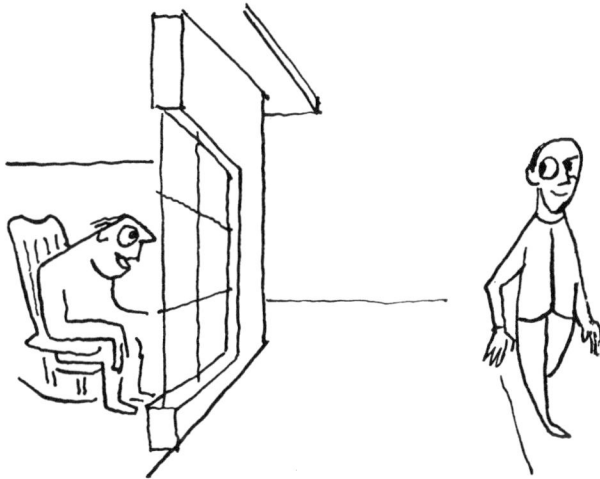

Windows are small in hot sunny climates to reduce the heat and glare; in cold climates larger areas of glass admit the sun's warmth. The windows facing north and east, since they receive less direct sunlight, are appropriately larger than those on the south and west.

We like to see and to be seen.

These variations in size have become less significant as climate controllers, because modern technology permits adjustments to be made by blinds, air-conditioning, louvres or shutters.

A window may be located to illuminate the centre of the room or the side walls. A high window allows light to penetrate deep into the room. A window close to or in the ceiling increases the amount of available wall space.

Windows are sometimes subject to conflicting demands. Small windows to ensure privacy may reduce the amount of admitted daylight and restrict the view. A regular arrangement of openings on the facade of the building may conflict with their proper placement in the rooms themselves.

The structural features such as lintels, arches, sills and jambs can be emphasized in the design to give the window importance - a kind of mascara in the architectural make-up kit. Windows in an interplay with the surrounding wall areas (solid versus void) create opportunities for a rhythmic treatment of the exterior.

Reaching out to catch the sun and extend the view, a bay window asserts its predominance over the wall while creating an extension to the room.

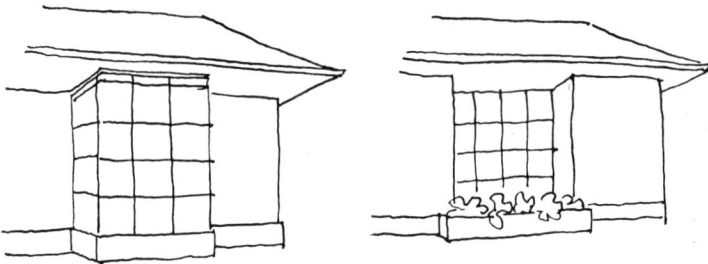

A recessed window allows the exterior to penetrate, while emphasizing the depth and solidity of the wall.

117

A window flush with the wall stresses the unity between void and solid. A completely glazed exterior wall takes over the entire facade.

The window speaks.

A tall narrow window suggests elegance.

A low squat one implies intimacy.

A windowless wall shuts off all communication with the outside world.

Like a stage director, the window can control the drama of the light entering the building - diffusing, focussing, coloring.

■ side light focussed on a church altar suggests a heavenly presence, especially if enriched by stained glass.

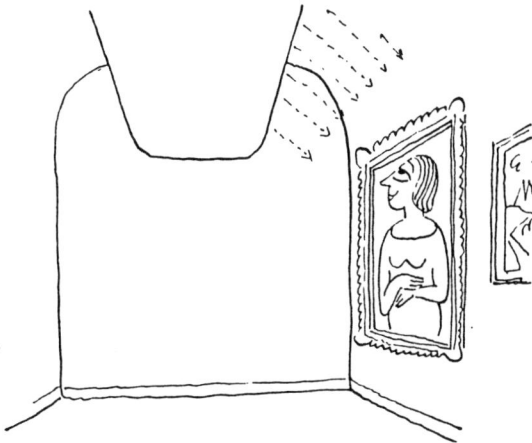

■ reflected light in a museum flowing gently over the paintings, provides a serenity to our viewing experience.

Thus the window is able to create a variety of light effects - functionally important and emotionally stimulating.

Space

Architectural space is infinite space broken up and manipulated to suit human needs. It is space with limits which establishes a controlled, protected, identifiable environment. Equally important, it provides an atmosphere designed to proclaim its purpose and establish a mood.

The first architectural space was "found space" - a cave, a tree, a projecting stone ledge. Later, space enclosures were built of natural materials, conveniently available.

Architectural space is meant for human use. Its dimensions relate directly to our own dimensions because it must serve both our practical and our emotional needs. It has the power to make us feel

120

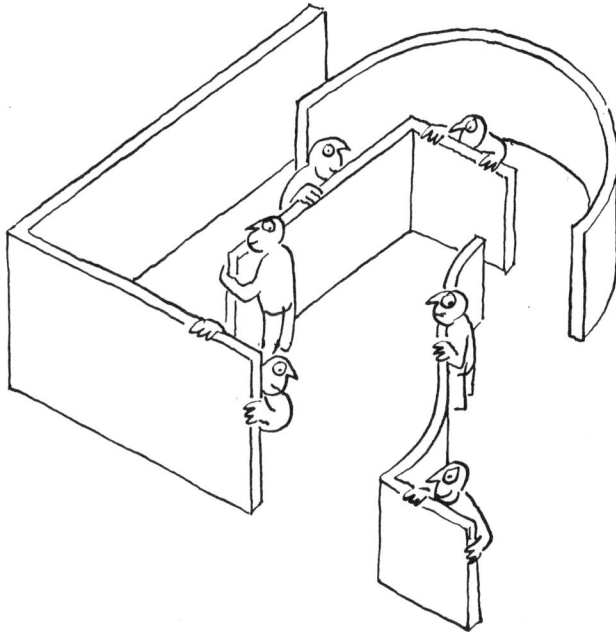

comfortably enclosed or depressingly shut in, liberated in its amplitude or lost in its vastness.

Because space can be given such a variety of shapes, the desgner has great scope in creating a wealth of moods. Space can be contained either totally or partially by walls, floors, screens, ceilings. The resulting shapes will be infinitely varied - conical, spherical, cylindrical, pyramidal or irregular. Spaces can be arranged as distinct units or run into each other in a constant flow.

An architectural space may also be an open outdoor area defined by buildings, fences, freestanding walls or lines of planting.

Shapes of space

Most architectural spaces tend to be "box-like" -

■ because the rectangular shape can most easily accomodate the furniture or equipment which the space will contain.

■ because the size and shape of building components become increasingly standardized.

■ because they facilitate the making of alterations, subdivisions and extensions.

The most self-contained spaces are sphere and cubes. They seem to shut out the exterior to place us at the centre of our own personal world. These shapes also tend to stop movement, suggesting the final destination has been reached.

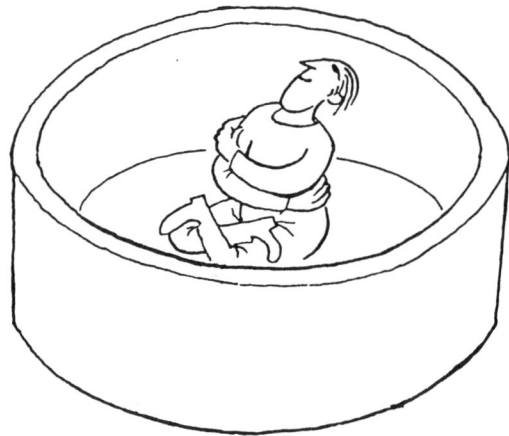

122

A semi-circular or parabolic shape, on the other hand, while focussing our attention, assures us of the possibility of escape by its open side.

Spaces can be contained within other spaces - a stage in a concert hall, a baldachino in a cathedral, a wedding canopy in a synagogue, even a boxing ring in an arena. Usually these contained spaces in the mother area are the focal points where important events are meant to be concentrated.

Space can also be layered - a mezzan-
ine overlooking a living room, a multi-
levelled shopping mall beside an **atrium.**

How we feel space.

Each of us defines space differently. We
all live in a sort of transparent bubble.
Some of us prefer large bubbles to encourage closeness with others, some
prefer the privacy of small bubbles.

A specific occasion may also dictate the preferred size of the bubble - small on New Year's Eve when "togetherness" is the order of the day, large on a crowded bus on a sweltering day.

Architectural space reflects cultural and personal preferences. The embrace of small spaces recall the safety of the mother's womb. A large space can suggest social, financial or political status.

A raised platform creates a semi-enclosed space which establishes the status of its occupants.

125

A recessed floor creates a semi-enclosure generating a feeling of in-timacy and cosiness.

A warm intimate space is appropriate for a tête-à-tête with one's sweetheart

A more ample setting is fitting for an encounter of diplomats.

A tall vaulted ceiling over a long narrow nave in a Gothic cathedral creates a feeling of spiritual loftiness.

Space can therefore be uplifting and inspiring, restful and enveloping or liberating and exciting.

Movement in space

We "possess" space by moving through it, usually from one area to another The voyage creates a sequence of effects, one space preparing us for the impact of the next. Organizing the movement makes the spaces effective, both functionally and emotionally.

Movement can be

■ continuous and rapid, the space flowing to a clearly visible outcome,

■ staged and gradual, interrupted by changes in level, detours, accentuating features, changes in light or other dis-racting devices - sort of a strip-tease, as in a department store.

■ from small to large or large to small to a planned climax. Rhythmic, alternating arrangements of architectural spaces - big and small, square and round, tall and low areas - to encour-age anticipation of the next area.

A large space will look more imposing by contrast with a preceding smaller one.

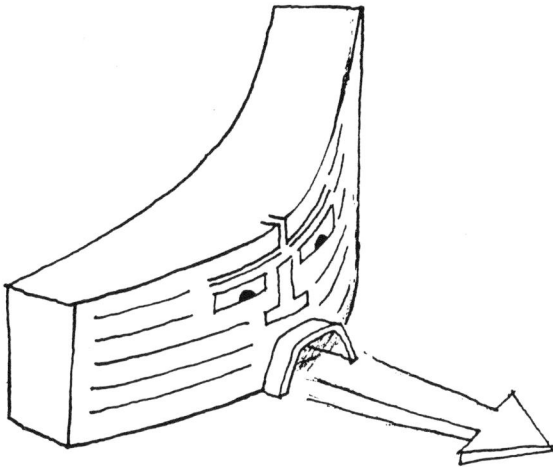

Possession of space

There is a relation between indoor and outdoor space - one seeming to covet the other. Interesting confrontations can take place between them. The shape of some buildings can seem to embrace the outdoors, or large glass areas permit the exterior to penetrate the interior.

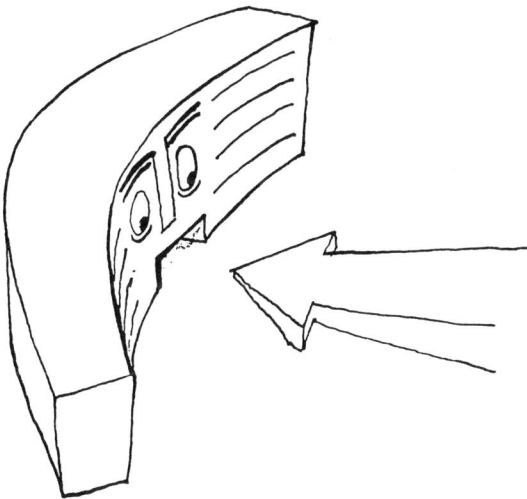

Manipulation of space

Space is not always real - it can be implied -

- by illusion - smaller areas made to appear larger and vice versa.
- by color
- by optical distortion
- by mirrored walls
- by floor or ceiling treatment
- by borrowing from an adjacent space.

129

Design

So far we have looked at buildings as users and visitors, Let us now turn to the designer of buildings - the architect, and see what may be the concerns and limitations involved in the effort to make a building function and, with luck, speak.

Architecture, of all the arts, has imposed on its freedom of expression the most restrictions. It is beset by a host of conflicting demands and limitations.,

■ The **location** will determine how the building will be placed on the site and how it will relate to its neighbors.

■ The **climate** will affect how the building will respond to heat and cold.

■ The **available materials** will determine the precise nature of the construction and its appearance. Large sheets of glass can make the building transparent. Steel will

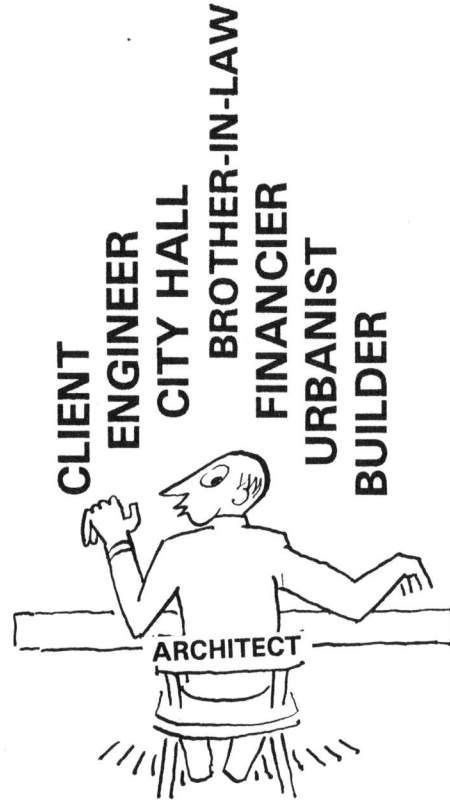

CLIENT
ENGINEER
CITY HALL
BROTHER-IN-LAW
FINANCIER
URBANIST
BUILDER

ARCHITECT

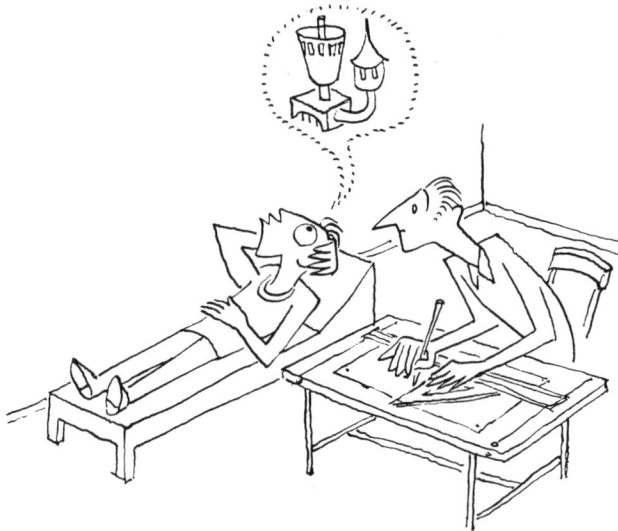

make the building tall and light. concrete can make it both malleable and rugged.

■ The **legal restrictions** will control safety of construction, ensure harmony between neighbors.

■ The **budget** will impose simplicity or permit elaboration

■ The **client** will put his individual stamp on the building.

■ The **technical know-how** will enable the building to satisfy new demands and take advantage of new methods.

All these stipulations are imposed against the background beat of the prevailing culture and the embellishing tremolos of current taste.

Their incorporation into the final design will involve specialists who will see the project in terms of their own exp-ertise and bias. They will make their demands and influence the architectural concept.

The architect is required to co-ordinate these specialties - town planning, in- terior decoration, lighting patterns, air- conditioning (in all of which he can hardly expect to be expert). The process involves evaluating and satisfying these areas of concern until they are all in harmony. The removal of even one item in the program can affect the whole balance and require a total rearrange- ment, if the result is not to be a patch- work. (Picasso said **"I proceed by a series of destructions."**)

The architect is trained specifically to conceive the overall idea and see it through to realization. He will try to exercise his baton-waving function by modifying, adjusting and often struggling to retain the logic, clarity and simplicity of his original idea. In the end he may be thankful to have been permitted an occasional aria of his own.

Above all else he will have to recognize and respect human strengths and limitations. We cannot stand too much sun; we are depressed by too much darkness; we can reach just so far for a cup on a shelf; we can only stoop so far to sit on a chair; we can only deal with steps of a certain dimension. Of equal importance - the architect will have to keep in mind that his aspirations to the loftiest spiritual and intellectual heights need not necessarily be limited by the standard dimensions of a plywood panel.

"An architect must be educated, skilful with the pencil, instructed in geometry, know much history, have followed the philosophers with attention, understood music, have some knowledge of medicine, know the opinion of the jurists and be acquainted with astronomy and the theory of the heavens." — *Vitruvius*

(from "THE CREATORS" p.102.)
— Daniel Boorstin.

WHERE IS A BUILDING PLACED ?

WHERE DO WE PLACE A BUILDING?

Where we are has a bearing on **what** we are. **Where** a building is, helps determine **what** it is.

Frank Lloyd Wright's "Falling Water" seems to have grown out of its site - interwoven with nature.

As the setting of a diamond can add to its brilliance, so can the site enhance the building. A convenient location, a happy relationship to the movement of the sun, a pleasant view, can all flatter the building. The building in return can honor the site.

The site

A building can dominate its setting or be dominated by it. It can be in contrast to the site or harmonize with it. A formal geometric shape will stand out against an irregular natural setting,

A Greek amphitheatre seems destined for its curved sloping site.

Conversely, a similarity of building to site through shape, color or texture will make for a harmonious blending.

A hilltop site gives a building a stature, a symbolic or political importance - proof of our mania to dominate our environent.

Mont St. Michel crowns its site and seems to grow out of it naturally.

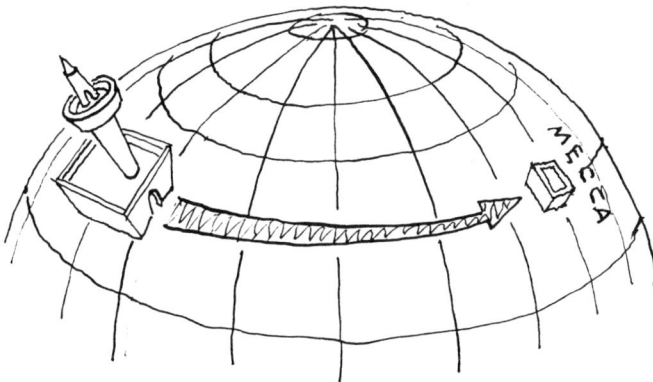

A mosque or synagogue will be oriented towards Mecca or Jerusalem, as a physical obeisance to the most hallowed shrine. The symbolism may take precedence over other factors in choosing a site - the shape of the lot, solar orientation, or ease of access; but choices must be made.

137

A plan suitable for one location can seldom be appropriately applied to another. Each site has its peculiarities which, if respected, can enhance the building. If ignored, can distort the design.

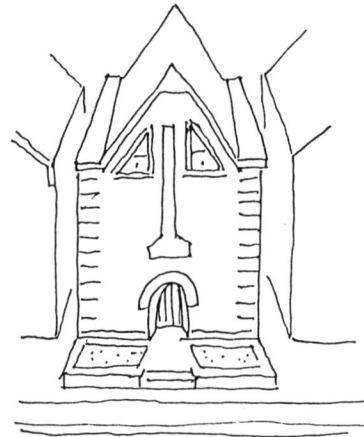

A building set on a large site will seem more important than if it is crowded into a tight space.

138

Invitation

An engraved deckle-edged wedding invitation, a phone call from the credit manager, an offhand "drop in and see me sometime" - each approach implies a specific kind of relationship. A building too can issue an invitation that will disclose the precise kind of relationship it offers the visitor.

The piazza of Venice seems to offer an open-armed welcome to the seafaring visitor.

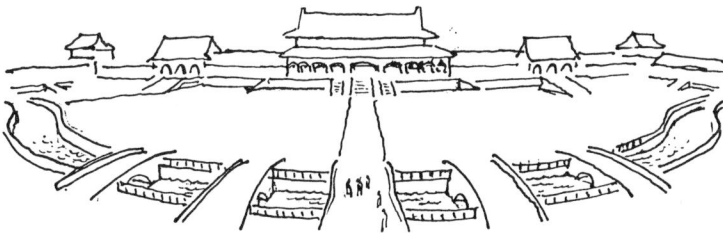

The forecourt of a Chinese temple cuts us off from the outside world before admitting us to its innermost secrets.

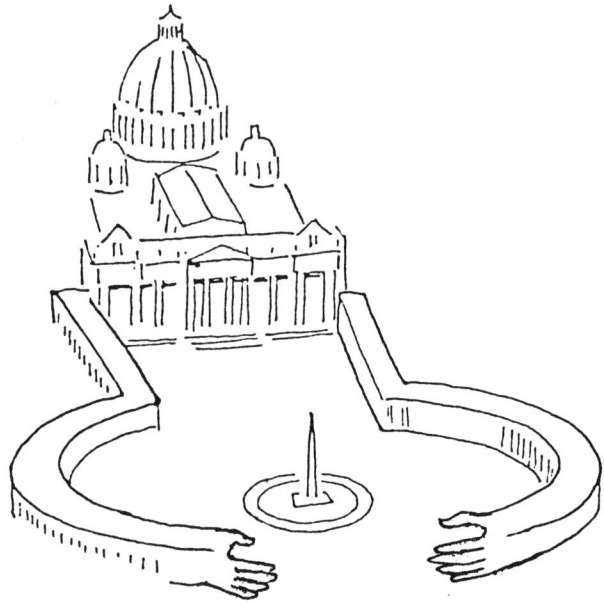

A curved colonnade before St. Peter's at Rome embraces the faithful.

A triumphal arched gateway warns us that our reception into the city is conditional on the acceptance of its power and jurisdiction.

The approach to the Campidoglio in Rome, from below, encourages a subservient attitude.

On the other hand the approch to the main square at Sienna, from above, confers on us a sense of domination.

A long straight avenue invites directly - but formally.

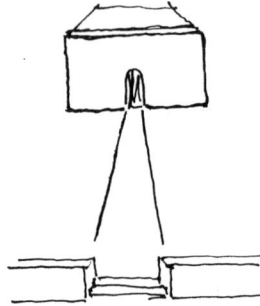

An immediate access close to the sidewalk demands no formal intro- duction.

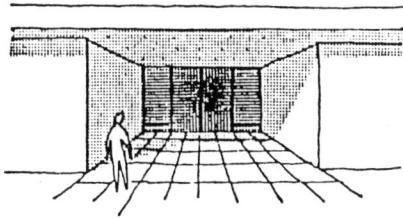

A recessed entrance suggests and even provides shelter before entering.

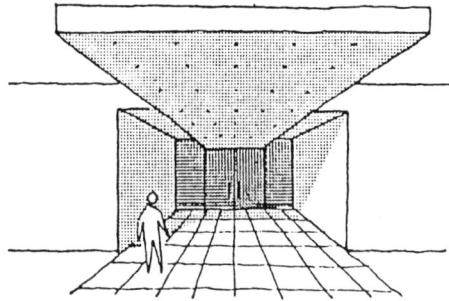

A projecting canopy reaches out to extend the invitation and helps to locate the entrance.

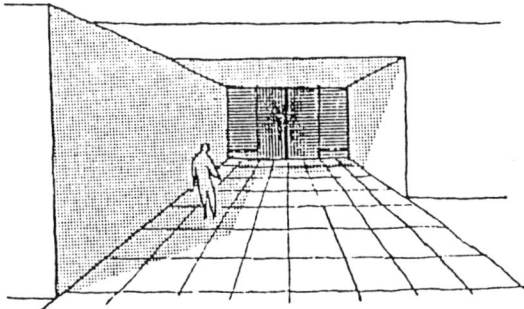

A projecting wall similarly stresses the invitation

An avenue of lights and a pattern in the paving add their welcoming touch.

Approach

The invitation to the building can be extended by degrees - from afar as a silhouette, partly revealed at closer range and finally bursting upon us - thus creating a series of suspenseful expectations before the final revelation. A similar experience can be felt while following the resolution of a symphony or watching the unfolding of a strip tease.

Getting there can be as exciting as the arrival itself !

A modest cottage may express its warm invitation by a simple ivy-covered gateway opening to a curved flagstone path.

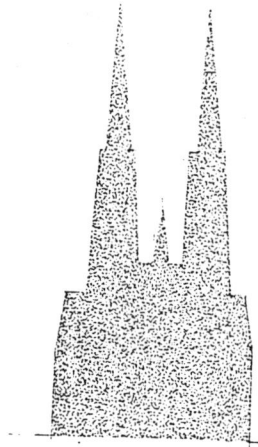

144

Identity

A building can speak by revealing its purpose.

This is a church. We know this because we have seen similar ones.

This could also be a church, but its shape alone is unrevealing, Its function may have to be further particularized by a religious symbol such as a cross.

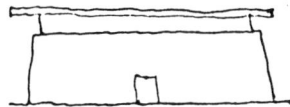

This could be almost anything. Its identity would have to be made very explicit by a sign, a logo, the owner's name, or a heraldic device to spell out its purpose. This happens to be a common situation because buildings serving different purposes often assume similar shapes.

Products sometimes impose their image on the building where they are manufact- ured or dispensed.

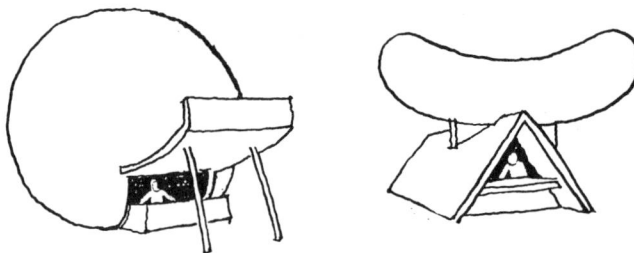

Signs, graphic symbols, flashing neon lights can gobble up the entire facade, transforming it into a vanishing back- ground. The street becomes a contin- uous billboard - an ubiquitous symbol of present-day city life.

The message has become the archit- ecture.

Manners

Morality is orderly behaviour - the acknowledgement that to survive we must respect one another's needs. Manners are a kind of enlightened self-interest. We legislate mutual rights and obligations or reach them by common consent. We become, to a degree, our brother's keeper. We try not to be too noisy after 11 p.m., we greet each other politely, we don't throw garbage onto our neighbor's lawn.

We are usually comfortable living next to a house not too dissimilar to our own. It suggests that our neighbors are like us, neither superior nor inferior (culturally or economically). A house sharply different in style might seem to suggest, to some, bad manners or poor taste - a disturbing intrusion into a well-balanced situation.

A hot-dog stand surmounted by a minaret
might be considered disrespectful.

Most communities do establish some
norms of appearance and function:

- "Roofs must be pitched"
- "Two-storey houses only"
- "No garages in front of the house".

But we are sometimes of two minds
about these restrictions. On the one
hand we may tend to be conventional -
afraid of differences. On the other, we
may feel that new problems or new
possibilities call for new solutions which
at first may seem inappropriate, even
outlandish, but for which the past must
make way.

The first garage at the front of the house was no doubt shocking and offensive, until its practicality was recognized and its appearance made to blend with the rest of the house.

City

If a building can be said to sing a song, a city can conceivably boom forth a symphony. Like the different movements of a symphony it can establish a variety of moods. It can evoke the excitement of a shopping or entertainment area, the laid-back feeling of a residential area, the controlled tension of a business district or the solemnity of a government compound.

The city can combine these various functions to make life easier, safer, more efficient, more amusing. By planning its spaces the city can provide privacy when wanted or contact with people to share joy, sadness or exhilaration.

What can a city say?

■ It can declare its main purpose (or its many purposes) - manufacturing? education? government? fishing?

■ It can celebrate its location - a seacoast, a protected valley, a mountain top,

■ It can celebrate an historic event.

■ It can reveal its concern for the welfare of its citizens by its parks, pollution and traffic controls, zoning regulations or public services.

Gertrude Stein once criticised the city of Oakland because "There's no THERE there!"

■ It can express its awareness of future needs in its planning program.

■ It can stress its dedication to special values by making its main squares and spaces the setting for symbolic or commemorative expressions.

■ If monumental in scale it can stress its political importance. If intimate in scale it can emphasize its respect for closer human relationships.

The street layout will reflect either a recognition of the nature of the site or a desire to impose an arbitrary pattern. Wide boulevards suggest a monumental outlook; narrow streets indicate a more intimate intent.

The voice of a small community with one main function can be clearly heard - a university town, a fishing village.

A street system winding its way up a slope (originally "planned" by cattle seeking the gentlest way) expresses acceptance and respect for the site's hilly nature.

151

In a large city, however, the many and complex activities risk creating a babble of tongues.

Harmony can be organized out of this prattle by grouping buildings of similar purpose - factories, stores, homes - into homogeneous zones. But oversegregation can result in entire districts being abandoned in the evenings or essential shopping services denied residential areas. Sensible mixes of functions are necessary to create both visual and functional harmony.

Each era sings its own tune. In medieval times the towering cathedral was central - physically, politically, ideologically. During the Renaissance the shift to temporal power made the civic centre the city's focal point. In the competitive era of private enterprise, office skyscrapers dominate our city cores.

Growth

Cities seem destined to grow and with increasing complexity and importance come a number of drawbacks.

- Cities once built for protection against the enemy without, now have to deal with the enemy within.

- Many city functions are moved to the suburbs and the city's central housing core is abandoned to decay.

- The population becomes segregated into economic strata and racial groups.

- Parks, meant for recreation, are now dangerous to walk in.

■ The street, once the living room of the city, has become a threatening thoroughfare. The honk of the automobile horn has stilled the smaller voice of the pedestrian.

It is not surprising that we have developed a love-hate relationship with the city. Its diversity, richness and culture attract us, but its dangers, overcrowding and pollution repel us. Nevertheless, there is a growing realization of the need to make the city less overwhelming and oppressive and more appropriately scaled to the everyday needs and activities of its residents.

WHAT IS A GOOD BUILDING ?

What is beauty?

I have tried to describe a building, its purpose, its components, how it is constructed, how it fits into its environment and how it presents itself to us. Now let us consider how we receive it, react to its impact and how we assess it.

Our first conscious response to a work of architecture is usually to say, "How beautiful! How nice! How pleasant!" or "Ugh! How ugly!". The response may be amplified or made more specific with familiarity. Generally our primary reaction tends to be an aesthetic one; and that now calls for a definition of a complex concept - **BEAUTY**.

Those things we highly approve of we usually call "beautiful".

The male rhinoceros, we can guess, sees **beauty** in his female counterpart.

The bee, we assume, sees **beauty** in the nectar-laden flower.

$$E=mc^2$$

The mathematician undoubtedly sees **beauty** in the order and pattern of the universe, and the pilot in the aerodynamics of his plane.

Beauty, it seems, can be found where something

- exactly fulfils its function
- displays order, harmony and pattern
- affords intellectual, moral and physical satisfaction.

Beauty is as beauty does - the reward for solving a problem simply ,totally, and elegantly. **Beauty = Excellence.**

"You get beauty without looking for it "
- says the engineer Candela.

"Architectural beauty is the perfect harmony of means and ends" - says the architect Van der Velde.

"If you work with geometry you have a better chance to have it look well."
 - Candela again.

Art is simplicity. It is what is left over when stripped of inessentials. ***"Less is more"*** - says architect Mies van der Rohe.

One may add that a structure that is seen to be adequate will make us feel secure - a valuable asset to aesthetic satisfaction.

Beauty varies with time and cirrcumstance:

- where food is valued, **fat** is beautiful;
- where food is taken for granted, **slim** is beautiful.
- where opulence is a virtue, **elaboration** is thought of as beautiful.
- where economy is a necessity, **starkness** and the bare functional may be considered beautiful.
- when order prevails, the formality of the **classic** is beautiful.

159

■ when freedom is treasured the play of the **romantic** is beautiful.

Beauty is a measure of current truth. Each era, time and society will define beauty according to its prevailing philosophy When the current view is challenged, a new definition will evolve.

Beauty is currently being redefined. A new awareness of the finite state of world resources and the need for a shift in our priorities, call for a re-assessment of all our values. The standards of beauty appropriate to a more affluent world apply no longer to a world in the grip of restrictions and cutbacks What we can foresee, therefore, is a shift towards an aesthetic based on economy and discipline.

Nevertheless not all buildings need find minimal expression. By common consent some buildings are exempted from such restraint. A great cathedral will merit the expenditure of effort, money, personal sacrifice and love. A government building, meant to fill the country with pride, warrants additional elaboration to properly fulfil its function.

Beauty can be found in the spare or the elaborate, but in either case efficiency and economy of means are important.

To survive we require a constant revision of our concept of ourselves and of our world. Our emotions and our minds interlock in this effort to learn what is basic for survival - when to advance and when to retreat, what to accept and what to reject.

An aesthetic for today seems to demand an increasing emphasis on ensuring our common survival. This understanding must stem not only from past experience but from an appraisal of current conditions and possibilities. From this assessment will arise a definition of beauty appropriate for today.

Morality and beauty

Can an ignoble purpose, even though wrapped in impressive visual trappings, result in a noble building? Can an art gallery, where the viewing of pictures is difficult, be aesthetically enriching? Can a stadium which threatens to bankrupt a city be considered a work of beauty? Can values, labelled artistic, transcend or deny social or moral responsibility?

It is considered by some that a work of art should be judged solely on its form, its technical ingenuity, its visual charm - that the content of the work is irrelevant.

The visual impression does certainly provide a clue to the possible presence of beauty. Orderly, regular, repetitive, rhythmic arrangements can be so persuasive as to make us forget beauty's other comp-onents.

A narrow definition of beauty involving formal qualities only, simply forces us into a limited and cramped view of civilized life and its possibilities, and consequently to a diminished, if not demeaning, role for the arts. This contradiction has troubled many. *"The ancient Romans,"* Voltaire complained, *"built their greatest masterpieces of architecture, the amphitheatre, for wild beasts to fight in".*

Does this limited definition of beauty tend to diminish art as a means of understanding and communication? Does it also leave us open to endorsing a notion which we may not wish to espouse, just because of its attractive packaging?

Yet it is easy to oversimplify, and hope for absolute answers. We are faced, for instance. with having to accept the Parthenon as "beautiful" although it was built by a slave economy. But there is no choice. Any definition of beauty must respect the limits of its own time and its prevailing morality. Pehaps the efforts to transcend the limitations of the prevailing culture rather than the actual achievements provide a better basis for aesthetic judgement. We must be happy with what was the best possible in the given circumstances.

Each culture must strive for a definition of beauty best suited to help that culture survive.

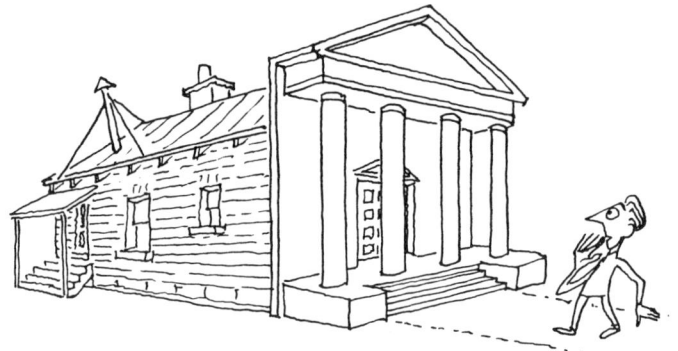

A scientist speaks of beauty:

"It makes you think of something solid, stable, well-linked. In fact it happens also in chemistry as in architecture that 'beautiful' edifices, that is, symmetrical and simple, are also the most sturdy: in short, the same thing happens with molecules as with the cupolas of cathedrals or arches of bridges. And it is possible that the explanation is neither remote nor metaphysical: to say 'beautiful' is to say 'desirable', and ever since man has built he has wanted to build at the smallest expense and in the most durable fashion, and the aesthetic enjoyment he experiences when contemplating his work comes afterward. Certainly it has not always been that way: there have been centuries in which 'beauty' was identified with adornment, the superimposed, the frills; but it is probable that they were deviant epochs and that true beauty, in which every century recognizes itself, is found in upright stones, ships' hulls, the blade of an axe, the wing of a plane"

" THE PERIODIC TABLE " - *Primo Levi p.179 (Schocken)*

163

Taste

Good taste is something we think we have, that we suspect our neighbors don't have. We are fairly certain that we are sensitive to visual and social subtleties in clothes, home decor or behavior; that we know what is appropriate, fitting, accept-able, well-mannered. However, to be on the safe side, we sometimes defer to those "experts" who may just possibly be more sensitive to the "finer" things. Our choice of a house, may be influenced by our sister-in-law or perhaps ordained by the current fad touted by decorator mag-azines. Taste cannot be equated with aesthetic judgement. At its best, taste may be considered a devotion to an elegant form of social morality; at its worst a timid retreat into the safety of the conventional.

Style

When an architectural solution, whether of a technical, functional or emotional nature, is refined to the ultimate and is accepted into the vocabulary, it has attained the status of a **style**. Style is seldom consciously devised. It is the result of relevant, repeated and finely honed solutions to a typical problem.

There are two main families of styles:
- the **classic** - rhythmic, stable, static, orderly, rational and respectful of rules.
- the **romantic** - spirited, dynamic, emotional, picturesque and improvisational.

Both attitudes - necessary for a full appreciation of life - compete for supremacy. They may contend simultaneously, or one may dominate a period to the exclusion of the other.

Style is not to be confused with trendy fashion or novelty, Fashion serves the need for variety and exuberance, but when our susceptibility is juggled by market manipulation and planned obsolescence, fashion becomes superficial and meaningless - lightly imposed and as lightly discarded.

When a society desires to define itself it may revive a style, hoping to recapture the admired attainments of a previous age. The recent craze for the so-called **post-modern** in architecture reflected a desire to be relieved of the preceding period's obsession with a purely functional "modern" expression in building.

Style unifies a culture or a place. Since technology and communication are now universal, diverse cultural patterns often interpenetrate and become international. Styles are sometimes copied indiscriminately whether justified by the specific circumstances or not.

Change

We are tugged by the past and lured by the future. The one cannot be completely denied nor the other ignored. The present is simply where the past changes into the future.

Basic emotions, it is true, seem to resist time and evolution. The tenderness of a lioness toward her cubs is as touching as the tenderness of our own mothers.

Sexuality, jealousy, ecstasy, agony are emotions we can appreciate as much in a Queen Nefertiti as in a Marilyn Monroe.

167

Yet we do resist change. The fireplace, long displaced by central heating, speaks too persuasively of home, warmth and togetherness to be readily abandoned.

The automobile, when first developed, clung to the shape of its predecessor, the horse-drawn carriage.   Even to-day, car designers, aware of man's nature, hesitate to make radical changes in their yearly models.

"Did'ja ever have the feeling that you wanted to go - still had the feeling that you wanted to stay?"

\- Jimmy Durante

However, a new form stemming from a new need e.g. a nuclear power plant, is more readily accepted than a too drastically modified car radiator.

New technical possibilities or political adjustments do generate new attitudes to our living arrangements.

The significant change in female attire in Victorian times was sparked by the growing independence of women. Yet change can also be superficial; witness the flip-flop from long to short skirts, and vice versa, manipulated annually by the clothing industry.

What brings about change in architecture? Economic difficulties in Europe following World War 1 swept away elaborate architectural ornament, to be replaced by a greater emphasis on honesty, morality and social responsibility. Taste became spartan, even in the homes of the rich.

More recently, economic pressures, greater mobility and the rapid increase in population have reduced the home in size and importance as the symbol of family stability. Steel and concrete have changed architecture technically and expressively.

At first a new idea may be exaggerated in order to be noticed. Only later will it be adapted to suit actual needs. But when it has been refined and generally accepted, boredom may ensue and the search for "improvement" may result in superficial embellishment.

Change may come gradually, or it may burst on us suddenly as an original insight.
- **original** not in the sense of being different solely for the sake of being different, but
- **original** in the sense of replacing an existing relationship with a more appropriate one.

Example: the toe-space which reduced the strain of performing a familiar task.

Judgement

How can we judge a building's merits?

Unanimous approval or disapproval of a building is seldom to be expected, for our judgements are affected by our previous experiences, and our individual "hangups" or prejudices.

"I know what I like," often translates into *"I like what I know."*

A tall building may frighten us; a low ceiling depresses us.

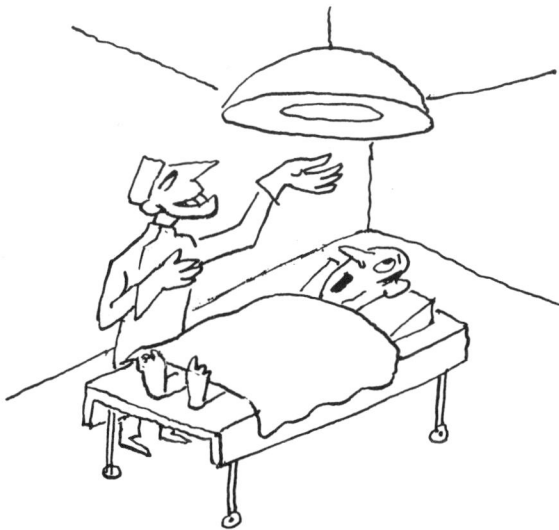

A surgeon may find his operating room beautiful; his patient sees only a torture chamber.

So it is useful to find some reasonably objective criteria by which we can judge the building.

- Does it fulfil its function?
- Is it structurally or technically sound?
- Is it suitable for the climate or location?
- Does it sit well on the site or in the neighborhood?
- Does it arouse awe, delight or resentment?
- Does it express a well-defined view of life - love of people, of nature, of complexity, of simplicity, of technical wizardry?

These questions may help us define our own feelings and beliefs about the building.

An unusual kind of building may be hard to judge. Its novelty may either excite us or threaten long-held notions. A new outlook may have to struggle through our resistance before we are prepared to extend an even grudging acceptance. Repeated exposure to the new may however open our eyes and mind and even lead us to change our opinion.

Can a building ever satisfy us completely? Can it approach perfection? However pure the original intention, a building's many competing elements and complex requirements may only produce a series of compromises.

It is true that the ancient Greeks sought perfection by subjecting traditional arrangements to infinite refinement. However our current tendency to find the

cheap quick solution usually precludes
the possibility of such a dedication .

A building has a pervasive influence on
us. Its presence is long-lasting. An unpleasant painting can be turned to the
wall - an unpleasant building can only
be avoided by going down a side street.

Interrelationship of the arts

All the arts of a given period usually have some common characteristics, because they reflect a shared world outlook. They all appeal to the same mind and heart, though they register on different senses - painting on sight, sculpture on sight and touch, film on sight and sound, architecture on sight, touch and even sound.

There are even similarities in the artistic devices used. The rhythmic arrangement of the window openings in a building facade may recall the rhythms in the notes in a music score.

No single art however can express all our reactions to life. The satire of a political cartoon can hardly be expressed in a building.

Sometimes the arts can be interwoven. The stained glass windows, the sculptured entrances, the pipe organ, even the aroma of incense in a cathedral are part and parcel of the structure itself. In the works of the architects Gaudi or Bernini it is difficult to tell where architecture ends and sculpture and painting begin.

When several arts are interwoven, they may compete for attention or express contradictory ideas - particularly in an age of individualism when conflict rather than harmony of ideas prevails.

Therefore the architect sometimes resists the intrusion of painting or sculpture into his building, fearing it may endanger the integrity or harmony of his design.

When the art is of an ephemeral form, as in "found art" or "happenings" or "self-destructs", their incorporation in architecture, which is dedicated to permanence and stability, can be difficult.

YOU AND ARCHITECTURE

YOU AND ARCHITECTURE

How responsible are we for what is built?

There seem to be two attitudes to this
question -
- What I build is my business!
- What I build, since it affects others,
is everyone's responsibility and concern.
Most frequently these contradictory views
are resolved by a trade-off - maximum
freedom within the minimum of controls.

However, the continuing overcrowding,
illogical use of land, pollution, traffic
snags and zoning irregularities - have all
exposed the need for greater concern for
the public welfare. This concern is not
always effectively expressed.

We do not often feel impelled or entitled
to interfere in building activity even in

178

our own community. Architecture, it must be emphasized, is not solely the sacrosanct preserve of the architect or the builder or the developer - just as military matters are too important to be left solely to the generals.

As the ultimate consumer of architecture, the average person, has a stake in the design process and his political clout can add strength to his opinions. The public should have the power to prevent, beforehand, the indiscriminate erection of buildings inappropriate in function or location. The best time to influence the process is, of course, at the planning stage.

Preservation

Our concern should also extend to those buildings threatened with demolition. A painting or a poem can be preserved in a museum or a library, retrievable at will, its spell revived at any time. A building however, runs the risk of demolition, to be lost forever if its continued relevance is questioned.

The temptation to replace an obsolete two-storey building in the heart of a city with a twenty-storey revenue-producing tower is understandable. All buildings cannot be preserved indefinitely. We cannot live forever in the past, but some tangible evidence of our history must be retained if we are to benefit from a unity of past, present and future.

We seek justifiable alternative solutions to demolition when we ask

- Is the building of special architectural significance?
- Is it typical of its time or culture?
- Is it important historically?
- Can it be re-cycled and adapted to serve current needs?

Architectural education

A culture is judged not only by its outstanding monuments, the achievements of its scientists, its artists or its statesmen, but also by the quality of its everyday life. We expect our art galleries or concert halls to lift us above our workaday activities and surroundings to more enriching and stimulating experiences. It is as important that our daily walk to the supermarket be, if not as exalting, at least free of stress.

A knowledgeable public is the best guarantee that the buildings and the settings where they live, work and play, or admire from afar, should truly reflect the highest ideals to which their society can rightfully aspire.

Our concern for the protection of our architecture and its environment would become more determined, knowledgeable and widespread if the teaching of architectural values were encouraged even at the primary levels of our educational system.

The future

The future of architecture is tied to the future of our planet. Depletion of natural resources, pollution, over-development, over-population, waste, greed have

transformed a world of plenty into a world of scarcity.

Basic shelter becomes increasingly difficult to secure, for many impossible. The search for new solutions to the problem is often abandoned as too difficult to solve. We have learned to live with slums - turning a blind eye to them, accepting them as somehow inevitable .

A moral uncertainty muddies our values, suggesting that architecture need only reflect life, not change it. This reveals a lack of faith in the possibility of achieving harmony in the modern world. In architecture this sometimes appears as a desperate search into the past for inspirational models, or a perverse celebration of disharmony. Some buildings even deliberately express instability and decay.

Moves toward new international political and economic accords seem to suggest that we may be ushering in a new morality, not as an abstract utopian principle, but as a practical instrument for survival - one which balances the good of the whole with the desires of the individual.

The architecture of tomorrow will be required to address the elemental problems of shelter rather than the search for "stylistic" superficialities. It is becoming apparent that what is considered beautiful can no longer be divorced from what is life-sustaining.

A new clarity of purpose will have to be combined with a unity of effort. Specialization has separated from each other the skills involved in construction . This has given rise to stereotypes: that the architect is an impractcal dreamer, the contractor or engineer a crass materialist. The future will be required to recognize that all disciplines working together with society (the client) are necessary for the complete and expressive realization of the buildings of tomorrow.

In this respect architecture, because it embodies so many principles applicable to other aspects of living, can serve as a good working model for understanding ourselves and our world.

Can we hope that our moral awareness may attain the same stature as our technical virtuosity and our commercial acuity? A yearning for some such unity may lie behind the poet Auden's all-embracing plea to *"Find new architecture"* in our lives.

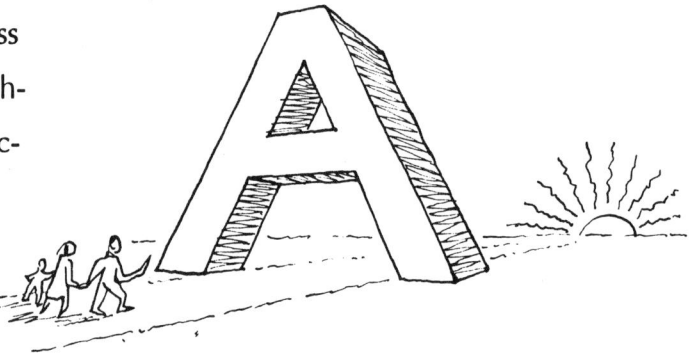

APPENDIX

In the foregoing pages I have attempted to describe some of the general considerations behind the impact of buildings on our hearts and minds. In order to apply some of these ideas to our daily experience of buildings we know best, I add a few simple examples.

In elegant books, slick magazines and on our TV screens, we are treated to the beauty of great architecture created by giants like Michelangelo, Sir Christopher Wren or Frank Lloyd Wright. But their actual work, scattered about the globe, is seldom accessible to many of us and its impact on us is, at best, secondhand. Our more immediate experience of architecture is with the buildings we actually live or work in - unpretentious or run-of-the-mill. Some are designed by architects, some by builders and others by their owners or occupants.

Because we are so familiar with these buildings we have stopped **seeing** them. We take them for granted. We sense their presence rather than consciously look at them.

It may be rewarding to examine them in a special way - by comparing a few of them with their neighbours. For this purpose I have selected in my own city (Montreal) pairs of twinned dwellings - semi-detached residences or double duplexes - which have been independently modified to reveal an individuality within a common base.

When seen side by side these modest units may reveal some principles of order and arrangement which we usually associate with more important architectural monuments.

The individual modifications or embellishments in each half of the building result from

- different needs - a porch, a railing for an ailing parent, a fenced-in area for the children.
- personal preferences or fantasies.
- the need to invest the resident with a visible status or distinctiveness with respect to the next door neighbor. Often much love is expended in these individual changes and the dwelling becomes an accurate and honest expression of the dweller's personality.

A

B

We find, in this pair of dwellings, the expression of two somewhat different relationships to the outside world. **B**, with an open lawn and walkway, issues an open invitation. **A**'s invitation is somewhat less open, "hedged" in by the neatly trimmed bushes which suggest a request for privacy. **B** wishes to call attention to the entrance by flanking it with two tall bushes. This arrangement may be counter-productive because the shrubs conceal some of the details of the entrance itself. **A**'s entrance, without additional emphasis, is more evident.

187

C

This pair of houses are identical in most respects. **D** has retained the original stone-work but **C** has chosen to paint it . The sturdiness of the original has been thereby light-ened, since the individual stone blocks and mortar joints are no longer emphasized and the whole facade is unified as an undifferentiated surface. **C** acquires even more delicacy by the alteration to the entrance, now treated as a single door set in clearly identified

D

white *transom and side panels.* The accent on the narrow separations between glass side panels and the doorway, also alter the scale of the building, making it look larger and bolder by comparison with the slim units. The whiteness of the whole front is further emphasized by its contrast with the dark bushes. However, these tend to conceal the sturdy columns which give in **D** a comforting feeling of stability.

E

The original version of this pair was evidently highly ornamented. Subsequent alterations have added to the elaboration. The complicated cornices have been accentuated by painting the swags in a contrasting color. The stark white of the window and door trim contrast sharply in E; a softer tone in F reduces the contrast and gives a more unified effect to the facade. In E, on the other hand, the balcony over the doorway has

F

been extended to merge with the bay-window cornice. While unifying it horizontally, it does strain the vertical relationship with the doorway. This axis has been strongly retained in E. The light tone of F's balcony and porch railings contrast with the brickwork, while in E the darker and thinner wrought iron railings are less insistent in size and color. This unity of tone reduces the busyness of the facade.

G

This pair of dwellings also illustrate a contrast in the color of the walls. The original state (H) has, in G, been changed to white with contrasting shutters. In G the contrast is reversed so that the whole double frontage has a lively checker-board effect. In G the extension of the porch and balcony (also painted white) blend with the brick wall (white) to create an overall unity. This is further

H

enhanced by eliminating the original upper cornice and its pilastered balustrade, which has been retained in **H**. *This latter element also helps to reduce the scale of that half of the building, giving it a delicately intimate feeling.* **H** *emphasizes the smaller balcony by contrasting it with the brick and, by this means, also accentuates the entrance.*

190

PRINTED AND BOUND
IN BOUCHERVILLE, QUEBEC, CANADA,
BY MARC VEILLEUX INC.
IN MARCH, 1996